OKOBOJI IOWA

OPEN 7 DAYS A WEEK ALL YEAR

Stadium Stories:
Iowa Hawkeyes

Stadium Stories™ Series

Stadium Stories:

Iowa Hawkeyes

Buck Turnbull

GUILFORD, CONNECTICUT
AN IMPRINT OF THE GLOBE PEQUOT PRESS

INSIDERS' GUIDE®

Text design: Casey Shain
All photos are courtesy of the University of Iowa Sports Information Office, except where noted.
Cover photos: *front cover:* Warren Holloway (© *Des Moines Register*/Harry Baumert); *back cover:* top, Chuck Long and Hayden Fry; bottom, Herky the Hawk
"Iowa Fight Song" lyrics by Meredith Willson. ©1951 Bourne Company. © renewed 1971 Frank Music Corporation and Meredith Willson Music. All rights reserved.

Library of Congress Cataloging-in-Publication Data
Turnbull, Buck.
    Stadium stories : Iowa Hawkeyes / Buck Turnbull.
      p. cm. — (Stadium stories series)
    ISBN 0-7627-3819-7
    1. Iowa Hawkeyes (Football team)—History. 2. University of Iowa—Football—History. I. Title. II. Series.

GV958.U526T98 2005
796.332'63'09777655—dc22   2005043448

Manufactured in the United States of America
First Edition/First Printing

To my wife, Jay, my loyal teammate.
She loves the Hawks, and she loves me,
sometimes in that order.

Contents

Acknowledgments

I would like to thank Phil Haddy, Iowa's sports information director, and his associate, Steve Roe, for their help and support. I would especially like to thank their secretary, Theresa Walenta, who searched the archives to help me come up with most of the photos in this book.

My computer guru, son Gary Turnbull, also deserves a special pat on the back. He led this old-timer away from the comfort zone of his electric typewriter and into the technological minefield of click and double click, left click and right click, upload and download, Microsoft Word, My Documents, Alt F4, and, of course, the invaluable Esc key.

I suffered only one crash, when a page or two went sailing off into thin air, but that was early on, and it quickly taught me the importance of saving everything to a floppy disk. I've become halfway computer literate—I even know how to send attachments—and now my typewriter just sits there all by its lonesome, gathering dust.

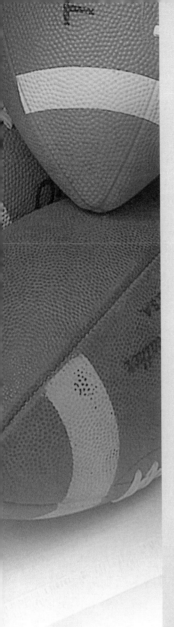

Four Hall of Fame Coaches

For just about one half the twentieth century—forty-five years to be exact—the University of Iowa was fortunate enough to have its football fortunes in the capable hands of four men who would reach the pinnacle of their profession—being chosen for the College Football Hall of Fame. While they might have had different personalities and coaching styles, all had one thing in common: They weren't afraid of challenges, working their sideline magic with amazing results when even the school's most loyal followers had all but given up on the Hawkeyes.

This was particularly true with Hayden Fry, most recent of the four to reach the coaching elite, joining the Hall of Fame in 2003. Iowa had gone seventeen years without a winning season before Fry signed on in 1979. After two more losing teams, Fry suddenly and surprisingly took Iowa to the Rose Bowl in his third season—and twice more after that.

First of the Hall of Fame coaches was Howard Jones, whose teams compiled a twenty-game winning streak from 1920–23, which is still a school record. Jones captured Big Ten championships with unbeaten teams in 1921–22.

Then came Dr. Eddie Anderson, who lifted Iowa out of the doldrums of the Great Depression with a turnaround that was even more sudden and shocking than what Fry would do. In his first year at the helm, Anderson was voted national coach of the year when he produced the storied Iowa Ironmen of 1939, featuring Heisman Trophy winner Nile Kinnick.

The Hawkeyes went through another down period during and after World War II before Forest Evashevski was hired in 1952. Evashevski's Hall of Fame career was relatively short but highly successful. He won three Big Ten titles and two Rose Bowl games in nine seasons.

All four men doubtless would have succeeded in other professions, but their love of football and passion for coaching led them in the direction they chose. The four did have one other very definite thing in common: knowing how to please the alumni. They won far more homecoming games than they lost. Jones was 6–2 at homecoming, Anderson 5–3, Evashevski 7–1–1, and Fry 15–5 including nine straight wins.

Fear Is a Great Motivator

Both Dr. Eddie Anderson and Forest Evashevski used fear and sarcasm as a motivator, and long after their players had graduated, some of them still held the two coaches in awe. Al Couppee, sophomore quarterback on the 1939 Ironmen, said of Anderson, "I had more fear of him than liking. He was on my case more than most because I was a quarterback and probably too cocky for Eddie's tastes. However, when he said 'Jump' I leaped. I learned to stay away from him at times, and most of the players went through this trauma in varying degrees."

Evashevski had the same effect on his players, if not more so. Randy Duncan, All-America quarterback on Iowa's 1959 Rose Bowl team, called him "a tough taskmaster. Everybody who played for him feared him."

One of the biggest stars Evashevski ever coached, All-America and Outland Trophy winner Alex Karras, didn't escape the coach's wrath and ridicule. As a highly touted sophomore in 1955, Karras let his weight get away from him and had a disappointing season. Evy began calling Karras "Butterball" and while it infuriated him, it may have been the motivating factor that turned him into a powerful defensive lineman. Evy later called Karras one of the best players he ever coached.

No Spectators Allowed

Howard Jones coached in one of Iowa's most unusual games, when armed guards were stationed at the gates to make certain no spectators were admitted to old Iowa Field. Because of the flu epidemic of 1918, health officials feared germs would spread in large crowds and said the game against Coe College could be played that year only if it were held in private. Reports were sketchy but there was general agreement that Iowa won, 27–0. The ban was lifted after one week.

Howard Jones

It is important to realize that the first forty or fifty years of college football were nothing like what you see today. Forward passing was not even legal in the early days, and when the rules allowed it—starting in 1906—the restrictions were so stringent that few teams even tried it. Raw power was the name of the game back then.

Coaches were mostly hired on a part-time basis and many were not paid at all. Howard Jones, who had been a star end at Yale, was a volunteer coach of the Elis in 1909. There were early signs of his greatness when the team finished with a 12–1 record and was recognized as the national champion. Jones spent some time at Syracuse and Ohio State as an advisory coach and then returned to Yale as the school's first paid coach in 1913.

Meanwhile, at Iowa, Jess Hawley was coaching the football team under terms of a ten-week contract in the fall while spending most of his time working in the investment business. There was grumbling among the fans that Hawley was not spending enough

Football Coach/Opera Singer

Iowa got much more than a football coach in 1898 when it hired Alden A. Knipe for the grand salary of $50 a month. Knipe, who had been a quarterback-halfback and captain of Pennsylvania's national championship team of 1894, was a physician as well as an opera singer.

Alden Knipe

In those early days of football, finances were a continuing problem, and after Dr. Knipe's first year it was announced that despite a net profit of $241.75 for the season, the athletic department still showed a total debt of $676.00. So before the 1899 season, the versatile coach decided to put his musical talents to work. An operetta, *The Mikado*, was performed on Thursday and Friday nights before the season opener, with Coach Knipe receiving rave reviews for his role as Ko-Ko, Lord High Executioner of Titipus. The opera house was filled for both performances and $381.60 was turned over to the university's athletic fund.

The football season also was a smashing success, beyond anyone's wildest dreams. The only blemish in nine games was a 5–5 tie with Chicago, which at that time was the premier team in the midlands. Coach Knipe's team also was unbeaten in 1900, winning the Big Ten title in Iowa's first year as a conference member.

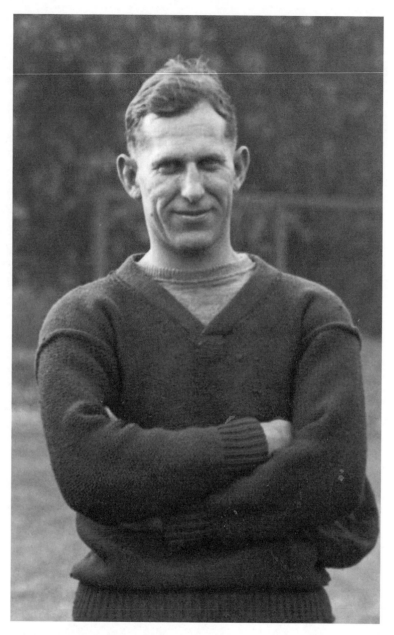

Howard Jones coached Iowa's team to perfect seasons in 1921 and 1922.

time on football, letting some of Iowa's prized high school athletes go to schools outside the state. Then the bottom fell out late in the 1915 season when Iowa suffered four straight lopsided losses to Minnesota, Purdue, Iowa State, and Nebraska.

Hawley said he had no plans to curtail his private business in favor of football, and with that he was released from his coaching obligations. Iowa then began the hunt for a coach and zeroed in on Jones, who was well known in the East, where college football was king at the time. The Hawkeyes offered him a five-year contract, almost unheard of in those days, starting with a $4,500 annual salary for the first two years, $5,000 for the third year, and $5,500 for the last two years.

There were certainly no regrets, although Iowa had one bad defeat in each of his first two seasons, getting whacked in 1916 by Minnesota, 67–0, and losing to Nebraska the following year, 47–0. Jones vowed he would never lose by such scores again, and he didn't. Those were the worst two defeats of his career.

In 1918 the Hawkeyes beat Minnesota for the first time ever, 6–0, and also shut out Nebraska, 12–0. It was the first of five straight victories by Jones over the hated Gophers, and Nebraska never scored another point on a Jones-coached team.

In the meantime, Iowa had started putting an emphasis on recruiting the state's top high school players, laying the ground-work for what followed. The Devine brothers, Aubrey and Glenn, came from Des Moines; a giant lineman named Duke Slater from Clinton; another good lineman, Lester Belding from Mason City; and Gordon Locke from Denison. They were the kingpins in the twenty-game winning streak, starting with the last three games of 1920, two straight 7–0 seasons in 1921–22, and three more in 1923.

Hall of Fame Coaching Records

At Iowa

	Years	Won	Lost	Tied	Percentage
Howard Jones	8	42	17	1	.708
Eddie Anderson	8	35	33	2	.514
Forest Evashevski	9	52	27	4	.651
Hayden Fry	20	143	89	6	.613

Overall

	Years	Won	Lost	Tied	Percentage
Howard Jones	29	194	64	21	.733
Eddie Anderson	39	201	128	15	.606
Forest Evashevski	12	68	35	6	.651
Hayden Fry	37	232	178	10	.564

One of Iowa's most notable victories under Jones was a 6–0 upset of a Yale team coached by his brother, Tad Jones, in the second game of the 1922 season. It was the first time a team from the West had invaded the Yale Bowl, and the outcome made front-page headlines in many newspapers across the Midwest.

After getting into disputes with the chairman of Iowa's athletic board and renegotiating his contract several times, Jones left Iowa in 1924 to spend one year at Duke (then known as Trinity University) and the remainder of his career across the country at USC. He won two national championships with the Trojans, who became known as the "Thundering Herd." Jones earned the nickname "King of the Rose Bowl" because his teams won all five Rose Bowls in which they played.

At Iowa, Jones's eight-year record of 42–17–1 for a .708 winning percentage still ranks as the school's best. Overall, his mark of 194–64–21 in twenty-nine years puts him among the all-time coaching leaders. He was still the USC coach when he died of a heart attack in 1941 at the age of fifty-six.

Dr. Eddie Anderson

Anderson was an Iowa native, born in Oskaloosa in 1900 and growing up in Mason City. There is a certain irony to that because the only defeat of his playing career at Notre Dame occurred when the Fighting Irish had a twenty-game winning streak snapped at Iowa in 1921. That would be the only loss for Notre Dame in forty games spread over five years.

Eddie was a member of famed coach Knute Rockne's first team with the Irish in 1918, and as an All-America end, he captained the team in 1921. Later he coached at Columbia College (now Loras) in Dubuque, Iowa, and then at DePaul University in Chicago while also earning his medical degree at Rush Medical College. From there it was on to Holy Cross, where his coaching ability flowered with a 47–7–1 record in six years.

Despite that glossy mark, his ties to Iowa were too strong to keep him from accepting the state university's coaching offer in 1939. Also, the fact that he could practice medicine at the nationally recognized University Hospitals was naturally a plus. Dr. Eddie, as he became known, would usually start work at the hospital about 6:00 A.M. and would still be in his medical whites in late morning when he'd show up at the football offices to shift gears for the day.

Dr. Eddie Anderson was voted the national coach of the year of 1939.

In those Depression times, Iowa's football teams were as sick as the economy, partly because the school had been suspended from the Big Ten in 1930 for using an outside slush fund to pay its athletes. Iowa did have some exceptional players in that era, most notably such backs as Joe Laws and Ozzie Simmons, but that wasn't enough. After the Hawks finished 1–7 in 1937 and 1–6–1 in 1938, the call went out to the doctor at Holy Cross.

What Dr. Eddie accomplished in 1939 seemed to be a coaching miracle. During September practices, when there were so few players with recognized ability, the *Des Moines Register* carried a short item noting "a set of iron men may be developed to play football for Iowa." Their nickname apparently stemmed from that, and they hadn't even played a game.

Hopes were so bleak that the father of Nile Kinnick, who would rocket to fame as the team's triple-threat halfback, made the long drive from Omaha to see the season opener against South Dakota, saying it would probably be his only trip and maybe the best chance to see his son play in a winning game.

Iowa did win in a 41–0 rout but that was just the start. Kinnick played one of his best games the following week to lead a rally that overhauled Indiana, 32–29. Anderson's Hawks were derailed at Michigan for their only loss of the year, and then they amazingly reeled off four straight victories, capped by a monumental 7–6 upset of Notre Dame and an equally unexpected 13–9 conquest of Minnesota. Both those November games were in Iowa City, and you can imagine the jubilation of the long-suffering fans, who celebrated for days.

Kinnick was injured early in the season finale at Northwestern, and the depleted band of Ironmen had to battle back to escape with a 7–7 tie. But that didn't take away from the luster of their accomplishments. Kinnick won the Heisman and Maxwell Trophies and was voted the AP's athlete of the year. Dr. Eddie, the man who put all the pieces together, was named the coach of the year.

Anderson enjoyed several more big victories: a 7–0 upset again over Notre Dame in 1940, and a 6–0 homecoming victory that knocked Wisconsin out of the national championship in 1942. After serving as a doctor in World War II, he returned to his coaching position in 1946. The postwar years were not as successful, and he returned to Holy Cross in 1950 to finish out a career that showed 201 wins, 128 losses, and 15 ties in thirty-nine years.

When he and his wife retired to Clearwater, Florida, in the early 1970s, Dr. Eddie sold his Amana Refrigeration stock that had been given to him by George Foerstner, founder of the Iowa company, as a reward for the 1939 season. He reportedly cashed out for more than a million dollars.

Forest Evashevski

When Evashevski came to Iowa from Washington State in 1952, the Hawkeyes had played only three winning seasons in sixteen years and hadn't won a Big Ten title since 1922. To say the outlook was grim would be an understatement. But out of such despair came a gigantic upset in his first year, an 8–0 whitewashing of Ohio State, and a number nine national ranking the next season. Big Ten championships followed in 1956 and 1958, after which both teams won Rose Bowl games, and then came another conference title in 1960. The 1958 team was crowned national champion by the Football Writers Association of America.

Evy had been a star blocking back for All-American Tommy Harmon on some standout Michigan teams before the war. He also starred away from the field, winning the Big Ten medal as the conference's outstanding scholar-athlete in 1940, and he was also president of his senior class. By the time he got to Iowa, he'd been the head coach at Hamilton College in New York one year before the war, coached with the Iowa Pre-Flight, served as an assistant on several college staffs, and compiled an 11–6–2 record in his two years at Washington State.

The rebuilding task was immense at Iowa, and his first season in 1952 started with four straight losses. Looming on the horizon was a home date with Ohio State, which had drubbed the Hawkeyes in the two previous seasons by scores of 83–21 and 47–21.

There is always hope, however, which is why they play the games. In practice, the week of the Ohio State game, Evy knew he had to make some changes and do something so his outmanned crew might at least keep the score close. What he did was completely revamp his offense, using wide spacing of the linemen to confuse the Buckeyes. Few teams had tried such a tactic before. "Ohio State used a standard defense and split right with us," said Evy. "They just couldn't seem to adjust to what we were doing. We gave them problems they hadn't anticipated, offensively."

Meanwhile, Iowa's aroused defense also thwarted the befuddled Buckeyes, who kept looking to the sidelines for help from coach Woody Hayes, but he had no answers. Iowa totally dominated the game for one of the most shocking scores in school history.

The Hawkeyes began to move up in Evashevski's second year, bolstered by many new recruits, and a 5–3–1 season ended in controversy at Notre Dame, which was unbeaten and seemingly headed for the national championship. Iowa also was domi-

Forest Evashevski coached Iowa to two Rose Bowl victories in 1957 and 1959.

nant in this game, and the Irish were forced to fake injuries at the end of both halves to stop the clock, saving time for touchdown passes that tied the score at halftime, 7–7, and again in the game's final seconds, 14–14. There were many who thought the ethics of the game, if not the rules, had been violated, and at Notre Dame of all places. When the Iowa team got home, Evashevski brought a roar of approval from students at a pep rally by offering this takeoff of a Grantland Rice poem:

> *When the One Great Scorer*
> *Comes to write against our name,*
> *He won't ask whether we won or lost,*
> *But how come we got gypped at Notre Dame?*

Several mediocre seasons followed before Evy installed a new wing-T formation, an offense full of deception and made to order for the talents of quarterback Kenny Ploen on the first Rose Bowl team and for speedy backs such as Bob Jeter and Willie Fleming on the second. Iowa football wouldn't be the same for the next five years, during which the Hawkeye record was 37–8–2.

Evashevski retired after the 1960 season, when he was only forty-two, to become Iowa's full-time athletic director. He could have kept the football job had he foregone the administrative position, but he chose the front office, leaving one to wonder how many more games Iowa would have won had he continued coaching.

Hayden Fry

When Hayden Fry decided it was time to leave his Texas roots and search for greener fields in the football coaching ranks, he made it known through the grapevine that he was interested in changing jobs. He didn't have long to wait for results. The year was late 1978. Three schools quickly showed interest and made their offers. Fry's problem at North Texas State was that after six seasons he didn't feel properly rewarded—especially after his teams went 10–1 and 9–2 in 1977 and 1978 respectively. None of the postseason bowls wanted to invite a school with little name recognition and a small fan following.

Two universities in the South were considered favorites to obtain his services, because he and most of his staff members had spent their coaching lives in that area. The third school was up north—Iowa of the Big Ten Conference—and even Fry himself doubted if his assistants would be agreeable to such a faraway move.

At a staff meeting, game films from the three schools were studied, and while Fry had not even visited the Iowa campus in Iowa City, he knew and respected Hawkeye athletic director Bump Elliott. Fry and all the assistants were impressed by the fan enthusiasm shown in the game films, despite the fact that Iowa had gone through so many years without a winning season.

Finally it was Fry's longtime friend and defensive coordinator, Bill Brashier, who settled the issue when he said, "Hayden, if we go to Iowa we can go to the Rose Bowl." Little did Brashier know how quickly that would come true. Fry took the Iowa job and brought most of his assistants, his Texas witticisms, and a wide-open style of football into the Big Ten. In 1981—only his third season at the helm—Iowa went to the Rose Bowl and followed that with two more trips to Pasadena in 1985, with a team that had been ranked number one in the country five weeks in a row, and again in 1990.

Hayden Fry discusses strategy
with star quarterback
Chuck Long.

A Fifth Hall of Fame Coach

Iowa actually had a fifth coach who is in the College Football Hall of Fame, but he's mostly the answer to a trivia question. Slip Madigan was not honored for anything he accomplished at Iowa—winning only two of sixteen games as a wartime coach in 1943–44—but for his long and distinguished career at St. Mary's College in California.

It's little wonder then that Fry became the most popular figure in Hawkeye history, wearing his familiar white slacks and sunglasses on the sidelines for twenty years, coaching ten ranked teams, and making fourteen bowl appearances. An old Baylor quarterback himself, he coached seven All-Big Ten quarterbacks in nine years. Starting with the Rose Bowl game of 1982, Iowa made eight straight bowl trips. Quarterback Chuck Long threw six touchdown passes to rout Texas in the 1984 Freedom Bowl, 55–17, and you know how much that had to please a certain square-jawed Texan.

Fry became noted for something else in addition to developing star quarterbacks: as a coach of coaches. Five members of his 1982 Rose Bowl staff became longtime head coaches. Kirk Ferentz succeeded him at Iowa, where he was coaching with great success in 2004. Barry Alvarez was at Wisconsin, Bill Snyder at Kansas State, Dan McCarney at Iowa State, and

Donnie Patterson at Western Illinois. Also, brothers Bob Stoops at Oklahoma and Mike Stoops at Arizona both played and coached under Fry.

When Hayden relinquished the reins at Iowa after the 1998 season, just shy of his seventieth birthday, he had coached the Hawks to 143 victories, by far the most of any coach in school history. He took a thirty-seven-year career record of 232–178–10 into the Hall of Fame.

The Legend of Nile Kinnick

One of the most amazing things about Nile Kinnick's legendary career at Iowa, followed by his tragic death in World War II, is the fact that his legend lives on in the record books more than sixty-five years after he played his last football game. Kinnick still holds six school records, several of which have been tied but never surpassed. Since he was a skillful and powerful punter, you might expect him to leave behind some almost unbeatable marks in that department. But what he did intercepting passes as the safetyman on defense borders on the incredible—or at least it's hard to believe no defensive player in the later era of specialization managed to outdo him.

Kinnick, who won the Heisman Trophy as the triple-threat halfback on Iowa's 1939 "Ironmen," intercepted 8 passes that season and 18 in his three-year career. Both have been equaled one time each, but so far no one has been able to dislodge him, despite playing many more games now in the modern age of wide-open football.

Kinnick was much more than an outstanding athlete. He was a Phi Beta Kappa scholar as well, president of his senior class, and a natural leader whose future seemed limitless when he graduated in 1940 with a degree in commerce. He spurned the professional game to continue his studies in Iowa's law school, although the Brooklyn football Dodgers made him an enticing offer. At the end of his first year as a budding lawyer, he ranked third in a class of 103.

With World War II looming on the horizon, Kinnick joined the Navy Air Corps reserves with an ambition to be a pilot if the world situation worsened and he was called to active duty. That call came on December 5, 1941, two days before the Japanese bombed Pearl Harbor and plunged America into a worldwide conflict.

Kinnick's letters home to his parents in Omaha and the journal he kept during his military service reveal the quality of person he was and why some of his teammates felt he was destined for greatness and perhaps even to be a future president. Such thoughts were not outlandish. His maternal grandfather, George Clarke, had been governor of Iowa from 1914–17, and Nile had

Tough Times

The success of Nile Kinnick and Iowa's Ironmen came just in time to rescue the athletic department from serious financial hardship brought about by the Great Depression. The university had not been able to pay interest on its stadium bonds for five years, much less any payments on the principal. Then, in 1939, home crowds took a sharp upturn and the bonds were retired after World War II.

his own political goals. He was a popular speaker at a few Republican rallies in 1940, and one Iowa newspaper, the *Marion Daily Sentinel*, announced that it wanted to be the first to endorse Kinnick for president—in 1956, the first year he'd be eligible.

During flight training in Florida, he was appalled by the terrible conditions that plagued African Americans. He wrote in his journal, "The inequities in human relationships are many, but the lot of the Negro is one of the worst. Kicked from pillar to post, condemned, cussed, ridiculed, accorded no respect, permitted no sense of human dignity. What can be done, I don't know. When this war is over, the problem is apt to be more difficult than ever. May wisdom, justice, brotherly love guide our steps to the right solution."

After attending a performance at the New York Metropolitan Opera House and hearing Marian Anderson sing, he left bedazzled and said, "Miss Anderson was dressed in a beautiful, full-length velvet gown of quiet green with a splash of silver extending

Young fans mob Nile Kinnick as he signs autographs in the stadium tunnel.

Iowa Has Retired Two Numbers

Nile Kinnick's number 24 is one of two numbers that will never be worn again by Iowa football players. The other is number 62, made famous for the Hawkeyes by Calvin Jones, an All-America lineman in 1954–55. Both men were killed in airplane crashes. The odd thing about it is that Kinnick was twenty-four when he died, and there were sixty-two people aboard the passenger plane that carried Jones to his death in 1956.

diagonally across the front from waist to hem. Her heartfelt rendition of 'Sometimes I Feel Like a Motherless Child' was marvelous. I could feel the moan and wail of the Negro soul echoing through the centuries. The perfection of her tone and interpretation swelled out over her listeners, and we closed our eyes and felt as if we were in church."

Then, after learning to fly, Nile wrote in one letter home, "I flew up in the clouds today. They were like a snow-covered mountain, range after range of them. I felt like an Alpine adventurer, climbing up the canyons and winding my way between their peaks—a billowy vastness, a celestial citadel."

The depth of his feelings and his way with words vividly illustrate what a learned man he'd become. He had a voracious appetite for books, especially about history: "Finished Sandburg's *Prairie Years* on Lincoln. Want to get started on *War Years* soon." "Picked up a biography of Mr. Churchill just recently written by Philip Guedalla. Read it straight through." "Finished Steinbeck's *Grapes of Wrath*." He said he needed some time to read the next one: "Started reading Tolstoy's *War and Peace*, the greatest novel ever written. It is 1,350 pages long."

Kinnick had been assigned to the carrier USS *Lexington*, which was in the final phases of training in late spring of 1943 before heading to battle in the South Pacific. It was cruising in the Caribbean, off the coast of Venezuela, when Kinnick took off in his Grumman F4F navy fighter plane on a routine mission. Some 10 miles from the carrier, another pilot noticed that Nile's plane was leaking oil. He warned him by radio about the trouble, that he'd better turn around, and he would follow him back to the ship. The oil leak soon became much worse, and Kinnick knew if he tried to land his crippled plane on the carrier, he would endanger other aircraft and the lives of sailors on board. He felt his only choice was to ditch in the ocean. "He was calm and efficient throughout and made a perfect wheels-up landing in the water," Ensign Bill Reiter, the other pilot nearby, wrote to the Kinnick family. Reiter said he saw Kinnick float away from the plane, although Nile might have been knocked unconscious by the force of the crash landing. Reiter radioed for help while returning to the carrier. When rescue craft arrived at the site where Kinnick went down, there was no sign of either pilot or plane, only oil slicks on the water.

The news of Kinnick's death shocked the nation. Iowa went into a state of mourning for the loss of a native son and a one-of-a-kind athlete. You couldn't have lived in Iowa in 1939 without knowing what this young athlete had meant to the university's football team, and how he had helped lift the morale of the state's populace near the end of the Great Depression.

Nile Clarke Kinnick was born on July 9, 1918, in Adel, Iowa, west of Des Moines. His father was a farmer and Nile enjoyed a happy upbringing, playing most sports and excelling in them. He was a promising baseball catcher, an excellent basketball player, and of course, outstanding on the football field. The economic downturn after the stock-market crash of 1929 proved especially harsh for the Kinnick family and Nile Senior lost his farm. He managed to find a job at the Federal Land Bank in Omaha and moved the family there (Nile had two younger brothers, Ben, who also died in World War II, and George). Nile's athletic success continued at Omaha's Benson High School and he was chosen on all-state teams in both football and basketball.

Meanwhile Iowa football was in the doldrums, partly because the university had been suspended from the Big Ten in 1930 amid charges that a slush fund was being used to pay athletes. The suspension lasted only one month, January 1930, but it had long-lasting effects. Losing seasons and lopsided defeats became the norm.

To the north, Minnesota had become a national power under Coach Bernie Bierman, who invited young Kinnick to try out for a spot with the Gophers, since there were no restrictions against such tactics in those times. However, Kinnick, who stood 5'8" and weighed 165 pounds, was not big enough or fast enough for Bierman's tastes. Rejected, Nile decided to cast his lot with Iowa because he was mainly concerned with getting a solid education. He tried to play his three favorite sports in college but gave up baseball after one year and basketball after two, giving him more time to concentrate on his studies.

Freshmen were ineligible for varsity athletics back then, and as a sophomore in 1937 Nile distinguished himself enough that he was picked for the All–Big Ten team, even though Iowa won

Nile Kinnick at about the age of six, holding a football of the times.

only one of eight games. Nile was injured in his junior season, which wasn't much better (1–6–1), and it was later thought that he had been playing with a broken ankle. Nobody knew for sure because as a practicing Christian Scientist his religious beliefs didn't permit him to seek medical treatment.

That brings us up to 1939, and it's easy to see why long-suffering Iowa was tabbed for last place in the Big Ten. The only apparent change was in the coaching staff, with Irl Tubbs being fired after those two dismal years and replaced by Dr. Eddie Anderson, an Iowa native with a successful six-year reign at Holy Cross. Dr. Eddie brought new enthusiasm to the Iowa players, and no one was more highly motivated than Kinnick.

Finally healthy, Kinnick wrote his parents, "For three years, nay for fifteen years, I have been preparing for this last year of football. I anticipate on becoming the roughest, toughest all-around back to hit this conference."

Probably the only person who would believe those words was Kinnick himself, but game after game, he made them ring true. The Hawkeyes warmed up with a 41–0 breeze past South Dakota in the opener, Nile throwing 3 touchdown passes, and that set the stage for his heroics to follow. On a sweltering September afternoon while playing against Indiana at Iowa City, the Hawkeyes fell behind, 10–0. That figured. Iowa had not beaten the Hoosiers since 1921. Then Kinnick went to work, playing his best all-around game of the season, scoring 1 touchdown and passing to end Erwin Prasse for 3 others. Nile totaled 211 yards rushing and passing while playing the full sixty minutes, leading Iowa's comeback for a 32–29 victory.

Michigan and All-American Tom Harmon derailed the Hawkeyes in their third game, 27–7, and by this time, still early

Nile Kinnick (left) with his coach, Dr. Eddie Anderson

in the season, Iowa's already-thin ranks were becoming even more depleted. Two starting linemen, Jim Walker and 270-pound Hank Luebcke (by far the biggest player on the squad), were lost for the season, and Coach Anderson began making position switches in an effort to plug the gaps. That's when the tag of Ironmen took on real meaning. A third starter in the line, Bill Diehl, went down and out in a 19–13 triumph at Wisconsin. Kinnick threw the winning touchdown pass to Bill Green in the closing minutes.

The Hawks had a small traveling squad on that trip, and Roundy Coughlin, a Wisconsin sportswriter, made this comment: "The Iowa bench last Saturday looked more like a high school squad. I don't believe they had one lineman to put in the game the last ten minutes." By comparison, he said, "Wisconsin had enough players on the bench to give Hitler another regiment."

A road game at Purdue followed and it was more of the same for Dr. Eddie's thinning troops, except there was almost no scoring. Tackle Mike Enich blocked 2 punts for safeties and Iowa won by the bizarre score of 4–0. Kinnick played his fourth consecutive sixty-minute game. Sophomore quarterback Al Couppee went all the way, too, and so did six of the seven starting linemen. That was when the Iowa fans knew they were seeing something special in the making.

"The one thing which will remain forever in my mind," Couppee said in his book *1939—An Ironman Remembers*, "was the welcome we got at the old depot in Iowa City when the Rocket roared in . . . I don't know how many people were at the railroad station, thousands probably. My sensibilities were not ready for the pandemonium which existed when I looked out the train window. I guess you could say we were all stunned. Nothing like this had ever happened in Iowa City . . . For the first time I guess we realized we not only had a record of 4–1, best in years for an Iowa football team, but we could win the Big Ten championship, and we could whip Notre Dame."

Wait a minute! Notre Dame was unbeaten that year with an eye toward the national championship. The Fighting Irish had lost only once in their last eighteen games. But Kinnick and the Ironmen did it again—Kinnick most especially with his strong

Nile Kinnick (24) scores the only Iowa touchdown in the Hawkeyes' 1939 upset victory over Notre Dame.

punting leg. He scored Iowa's only touchdown on a line plunge in the second quarter and then dropkicked the crucial extra point. Notre Dame missed what would have been a tying conversion kick in the second half and Iowa held on to win, 7–6. Kinnick's punting that day was a performance for the ages. His 16 punts totaled a Big Ten record 731 yards.

Nile kept kicking the Hawks out of danger. Late in the game, with the ball on Iowa's 38 yard line, he added the final dagger in the Irish heart, a high punt that soared over the safety's head and out of bounds at the Notre Dame 6. "I knew at that precise moment that we had whipped Notre Dame," Couppee said. "It was the single most exhilarating, thrilling moment in all my football life."

The Iowa campus and Iowa City's downtown area were overrun by joyous students, and the university president joined in the celebration by calling off classes Monday and ordering that arrangements be made for a victory dance in the Memorial Union that afternoon. Monday was Dr. Eddie's fortieth birthday, and he even gave his players the day off to take part in the festivities.

The final home game of this storybook season was immediately ahead, against archrival Minnesota, which had won the national championship in 1936 and would win two more in 1940 and 1941. The Gophers had drubbed Iowa in Kinnick's first two years, 35–10, and 28–0.

Chances did not look good for the undermanned Hawkeyes, and they went into the last quarter trailing the Gophers, 9–0. Did Kinnick have any magic left? Yes. He waited until the fourth quarter and then got Iowa on the board with a short scoring pass to Prasse. Nile's dropkick for the extra point cut the deficit to 9–7. Then, with about five minutes to go, the Hawks took the ball after a punt at their 21 yard line and Kinnick's running and passing guided them downfield; his 28–yard touchdown pass to Bill Green produced a stunning final score of 13–9. Naturally, another wild celebration ensued. Some said it lasted for days. "IOWA CITY GOES MAD WITH JOY," screamed a banner headline in the *Des Moines Register*.

Last of the Dropkickers

Dropkicking became a lost art in the 1930s when the football was streamlined to encourage passing. The pointed ball made it much more difficult to time the drop and the kick for any degree of success. However, Kinnick had mastered the technique, continuing to use it for extra points when others had given up. Kinnick is believed to be the last of the full-time dropkickers. Now conversions and field goals are almost always kicked using a holder to place the ball.

Not even a 7–7 tie in the finale at Northwestern, when Kinnick was injured and unable to play in the second half, rubbed any luster from the Hawkeyes' accomplishments. Kinnick was everybody's All-American and he won just about every award possible: the Heisman Trophy, the Maxwell award, and the Walter Camp Trophy, all signifying his place as the number one player in the country. He also was named the Associated Press male athlete of the year ahead of two men who were no ordinary Joes: Joe DiMaggio and Joe Louis.

Kinnick's Heisman Trophy acceptance speech was a classic and brought a standing ovation from the audience at New York's Downtown Athletic Club when he closed by saying, "I thank God I was warring on the gridirons of the Midwest and not on the battlefields of Europe. I can speak confidently and positively that the football players of this country would much rather struggle and fight to win the Heisman award than the Croix de Guerre."

Nile Kinnick takes a practice punt under the watchful eye of assistant coach Frank Carideo.

As another sign of his popularity, Kinnick was the top vote-getter in a poll to pick the College All-Stars for their annual game in Chicago against the professional champions, this time the Green Bay Packers, in the summer of 1940. Kinnick passed for 2 touchdowns and dropkicked 4 extra points, but the Packers prevailed, 42–28.

The Brooklyn Dodgers had drafted Kinnick but couldn't induce him to play. Even Dan Topping, the owner, made a trip

Nile Kinnick proudly holds his Heisman Trophy in 1939.

to Iowa City and brought his famous wife, figure skater Sonja Henie, to meet with the Hawkeye star over dinner. Kinnick invited several teammates to join him, but he politely declined Topping's $10,000 offer, saying he had played his last football game and now was off to law school.

In addition to his two school records for season and career pass interceptions, Kinnick still holds other school marks for punt returns in a game (9) and yards returned (201) against Indiana in 1939. But it's those punting figures in the Notre Dame game that are so mind-boggling. Sixteen kicks for an astounding 731 yards figure out to a 45.6-yard average. The 731 is still an all-time Big Ten record, and you have to think it will never be broken. That would be a perfect legacy for the memory of Nile Kinnick—a record that lasts forever.

Kinnick Stadium

When Iowa built its football stadium in 1929—completing it in just seven months from spring to fall—the timing was good in one way but horrendous in another. Good because had it not been constructed at that time to replace an inadequate field on the east side of the Iowa River, it might have been years before the university would be able to make such a financial commitment. Not so good because less than a week after

Pink Walls for Visitors

When Hayden Fry took over as Iowa's head coach, he decided to use a psychological ploy to play with the minds of visiting teams. He had the opponents' locker room walls in Kinnick Stadium painted pink, a passive and calming color.

Did it work? Well, at least two coaches, Bo Schembechler of Michigan and Mike White of Illinois, voiced their displeasure to Fry. Schembechler was so annoyed that he had his student managers cover the walls with white paper.

"Pink is often found in girls' bedrooms," explained Fry, "and some consider it a sissy color. When I talk with coaches on the field before a game and they mention the pink walls, I know I've got 'em."

That was sure true in 1985. After Schembechler complained, his Michigan team lost a 12–10 thriller in Kinnick Stadium. Later that same year White saw his Fighting Illini get thumped there, 59–0.

Iowa played the dedication game in its new 42,500-seat stadium came Black Thursday and the stock market crash of 1929. The nation was plunged into the Great Depression that would last for the next decade.

Further compounding Iowa's problems, the Hawkeye athletic department was under investigation by the Big Ten Conference on charges that the university was paying its athletes. There were suspicions about how the school had gained the services of several football players, including an outstanding running back named Mayes McLain, who joined the team in 1928 after transferring from the Haskell Institute (a school in Kansas for Native Americans). As an outgrowth of all this, athletic director Paul Belting, the man mostly responsible for getting the stadium plans approved, resigned under fire on April 26, 1929. The $500,000 stadium project was barely under way.

The Big Ten's probe into the athletic affairs lasted several months, but in late 1929 it was announced that Iowa had been suspended from the conference for one year, or until the university got its house in order. The suspension lasted only thirty-one days—January 1930—but irreparable harm was done to Iowa's athletic program. The Hawkeyes had to put together a makeshift schedule for the 1930 season when only one conference member, Purdue, would agree to play them. As a result football income plummeted to only $42,000 that year, compared to an all-time high of $200,000 in 1929.

Good athletes who might otherwise have gone to Iowa shunned the school, and the continuing tough economic times made it doubtful that the university would have been able to build what was then called Iowa Stadium—it was later named for Nile Kinnick—had the circumstances not been just right in 1929.

Athletic director Belting announced plans for the stadium construction at a pep rally on October 26, 1928. It was to be built directly west of the university's large field house, which had just been completed and dedicated the year before. A $500,000 bond issue was sold, yielding 5 percent interest according to the prospectus and to be paid off in the next thirteen years with athletic department revenue.

The Good Old Days

The price for a ticket to see the first two Iowa football games in 1929 was only one dollar, double the cost of a movie at that time. After the Hawkeyes moved from old Iowa Field and began playing Big Ten opponents in their new stadium, prices jumped to three dollars for games against Illinois and Minnesota.

Plans were drawn by Proudfoot, Rawson, and Souers of Des Moines, who had designed many university buildings on the east and west sides of the Iowa River including the field house, at that time billed as "the largest building of its kind in the world." The stadium was to consist of two concrete grandstands seating about 21,000 on each side, going seventy-nine rows high and running from goal line to goal line. The general contractor for the project was the Tanager Construction Company of Albert Lea, Minnesota.

Groundbreaking ceremonies took place on March 6, 1929, but there were almost immediate problems when excavation work began to lower the playing field about 30 feet. Teams of horses and mules were bought in to move the dirt, with scoops operated by the driver (no bulldozers in those days). Underground wells kept popping up, seeping water into the clay, and coupled with spring rains the building site was a continual quagmire.

When a horse or mule got stuck in the mud, another team would be hitched on to pull them out. Sometimes the animals

Stadium construction work was rushed to completion from spring to fall 1929.

would be overcome and die from the heat and exhaustion or break a leg and have to be destroyed, and there was no easy way to haul them out. Instead, the workers simply buried them under what are now the north grandstands.

Shifts operated twenty-four hours a day from March to July, with some 300 men employed on the project constantly coming and going. Figures for the material it took to erect the stadium grandstands are mind-numbing: seventeen million pounds of sand, more than six million pounds of cement (64,000 ninety-four-pound bags), and an untold number of bricks to make the outside of the structure compatible with the field house and nearby University Hospital.

"Major supplies, other than sand, came primarily by rail and were unloaded on a Rock Island Railroad siding directly south of the stadium, and hauled directly north on a street to the stadium," recalled Irving Weber, an Iowa City historian. "The siding had been used two years earlier when the field house was built and the preceding year when the hospital was constructed." That rail line was used for many years to transport fans to the games from Des Moines and points west. After that was discontinued several decades back, the university started using it again in 2004 as a shuttle service running from the nearby Coral Ridge Mall to help alleviate traffic congestion.

When completed, the stadium was the only one in the Big Ten that was half above the ground and half below, and it was also the only one where the seats were "dished." The first forty-one rows of seats all went back at the same angle, the remaining thirty-eight rows at a steeper angle so the top rows would not be as far from the field as they would have been otherwise.

The actual cost of the stadium was $497,151.42, which certainly was a bargain-basement price tag compared to rising costs due to inflation as the seating capacity gradually increased over the years to 70,000. When a new three-story press box went up in 1958, the bill was almost as much as the original stadium—$490,628.82; and a current two-year renovation job is projected to cost $87 million.

Although the stadium's construction was nearly finished in late September 1929, it was decided to play the first home game

He Who Hesitates . . .

How tough was it in the Great Depression? Well, after Indiana played a game at Iowa in 1931, the Hoosiers were sent a check for $8,563.18 as their share of the gate. But they didn't cash it promptly and when they tried, it was worthless. The First National Bank of Iowa City, on which the check was drawn, had failed.

of the season on old Iowa Field. The Hawkeyes easily beat Carroll College of Wisconsin, 46–0. Then came a shakedown game in the new stadium against Monmouth College of Illinois, with captain Willis Glassgow making history by scoring the first touchdown on a 30-yard run. Oddly, that result also was 46–0.

The same bad weather that had plagued construction workers also marred the dedication game, a 7–7 tie with Illinois on Saturday, October 19. It rained all day Friday and most of Saturday, creating a muddy mess. Sec Taylor was on hand for the *Des Moines Register* and he wrote, "An estimated 36,000 persons packed into the stadium, making a human-walled, varicolored canyon, at the bottom of which was the gridiron. Oil cloth blankets, raincoats, and sweaters of bright colors, however, quickly faded into the drab of a soggy, reeking afternoon, for the light sprinkle which fell as the homecomers gathered, at the finish had reached the proportions of a downpour."

Although the new two-sided structure made the construction target date on time, no landscaping had been done on the outside. The only way for spectators to reach the stands was on a pair of narrow boardwalks—one on the east side and one on the west. This proved adequate before the game but caused major problems as the fans left all at once afterwards.

Eric Wilson, a former longtime sports information director at Iowa, recalled the conditions this way: "Either side of that board sidewalk was a sea of mud. Occasionally when a lady would be accidentally bumped off the boardwalk, she would be pulled back to safety, but minus her slippers, which were irretrievably engulfed deep down in the mud. Ladies' slippers were surfacing from their burial ground for the next several years."

The rainy game got off to a roaring start for Iowa with Glassgow racing 78 yards to a touchdown on the very first play. His extra-point kick hit the crossbar and luckily bounced up and over, giving Iowa a 7–0 lead. Illinois tied it in the second quarter on a busted play, when the center mistakenly passed the ball to Doug Mills, who ran one way while his interference was going in the other direction. The play so confused Iowa that Mills was able to run for the tying touchdown, but that was it. Neither team scored again.

Illinois coach Bob Zuppke, who was one of the more inventive men of that era, saw great possibilities in the way Mills had scored. He added the play to his playbook for future games, and that's how the "naked reverse" came into being.

Iowa had only one other home game that year, posting a 9–7 victory over old nemesis Minnesota on Oran "Nanny" Pape's last-minute touchdown, finishing the season with a 4–2–2 record. But tough economic times were ahead, of course, and there was little to cheer about for the Hawkeyes until Nile Kinnick and the 1939 Ironmen came to the rescue.

Willis Glassgow ran 78 yards to a touchdown on the first play of Iowa's dedication game in 1929.

Kinnick Stadium Timeline

1929: Construction begins on March 8.

1930–39: Wooden bleacher seats were gradually added to the north and south end zones, increasing capacity to 50,000.

1946: Another expansion in the south end zone raises seating capacity to 53,000.

1956: The first major expansion is completed, adding permanent seats in the south end zone and increasing capacity to 60,000.

1958: A three-floor press box is added, extending between the 25 yard lines and replacing smaller press boxes on each side of the stadium.

1972: An artificial surface is installed to replace the grass field. The name is changed from Iowa Stadium to Nile Kinnick Stadium, honoring the memory of the school's only Heisman Trophy winner, who died in World War II.

1981: The artificial field is replaced with a new one.

1983: The north end zone is enclosed, raising capacity to 70,397.

1985: A fourth floor is added to the press box.

1989: A new field of natural grass, called Prescription Athletic Turf, replaces the artificial surface.

1995–99: The press box undergoes a $3 million renovation, including the addition of eighteen private viewing suites and remodeling of the facility into five levels.

1997: A large video display unit is added to the scoreboard system, allowing spectators to see live action, instant replays, and other features.

2004–06: An $87 million renovation is planned to include new south stands to blend in with the rest of the brick structure, a new press box running from goal line to goal line, construction of club seating, and forty-seven luxury suites.

An aerial view of Kinnick Stadium, packed with fans for a Hawkeyes game.
University of Iowa Photo Service

After Kinnick's death there was a postwar clamor to rename Iowa Stadium in his memory. It probably would have been done at that time except that Nile Kinnick senior objected to singling out his son in such a manner. He pointed out that many others lost sons in the war, including a second of his three sons. Younger brother Ben, a Marine fighter pilot, was shot down and killed in the South Pacific in late 1944.

In 1972 the elder Kinnick, who would live well into his nineties, finally relented and agreed to the name change. It officially became Nile Kinnick Stadium on September 23, 1972, in a pregame ceremony before Iowa played Oregon State. Nile senior was there and took part in the festivities for a lasting tribute to his son.

Over the years there have been many rousing victories in Kinnick Stadium, some great individual performances, and more than a few bitter disappointments. There have also been some unusual incidents. Such as the time a young male "streaker" raced across the playing field, displaying his nakedness to the amusement of some 60,000 fans who otherwise had little to cheer about on that long-ago afternoon. It happened before a 1974 game against Penn State, and as it turned out he made the longest run of the day before being nabbed by security guards, because the Hawkeyes lost, 27–0, and didn't make so much as a first down in the first three quarters.

Then there was the time a referee lost track of the downs late in a 1963 game against Washington State. He turned the ball over to Iowa instead of giving the Cougars a fourth down and a chance to go for a game-winning field goal. Instead, the teams ended in a 14–14 tie.

Or the time in the 1960s when a public-address announcer made derogatory remarks about an athletic department staff member on the field below, not realizing his microphone was in the on position. That was his last game at the mike. He was fired the next week.

And then there is the fact that the stadium is a burial ground in more ways than one, and not just for horses and mules. The southwest corner of the main structure is a cemetery of another sort: Several thousand parachutes were disposed of deep in the ground at that location, the result of a military surplus bargain purchase that went awry. An assistant athletic director of that bygone era came up with the idea of using parachute material as a cheap way to cover fences on the football practice fields, but when it came time to test his theory, the parachutes proved both impractical and ugly. Getting rid of the evidence underneath the stadium became a summer work project for several varsity athletes.

There's no telling what future renovation projects might unearth. Maybe a few animal bones or a parachute—or even some ladies' slippers.

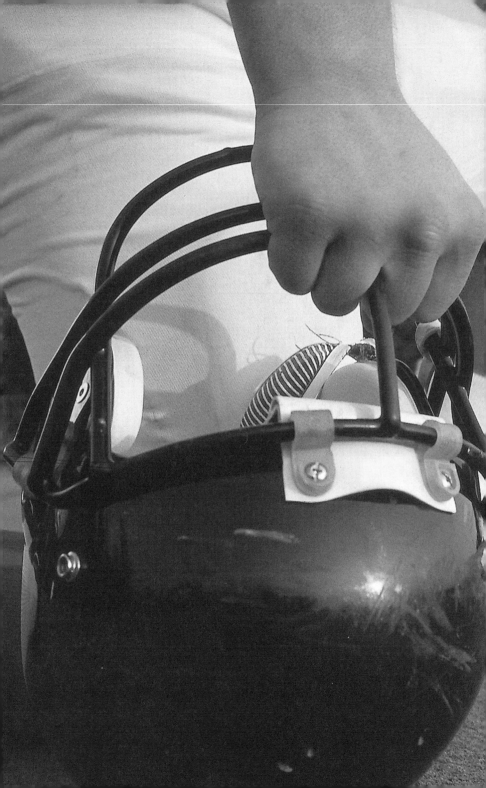

Hawkeye Stars

No one expected the kind of spectacular season that quarterback Brad Banks would enjoy in 2002, which made what he did all the more memorable in leading the Hawkeyes to an unbeaten Big Ten cochampionship and into the Orange Bowl. Banks threw at least 1 touchdown pass in all thirteen games. He threw at least 2 in seven of the eight conference games, and his marksmanship was so good that he topped the nation in

2002 Big Ten Standings

	Wins	Losses	Ties
Iowa	8	0	0
Ohio State	8	0	0
Michigan	6	2	0
Penn State	5	3	0
Purdue	4	4	0
Illinois	4	4	0
Minnesota	3	5	0
Wisconsin	2	6	0
Michigan State	2	6	0
Indiana	1	7	0
Northwestern	1	7	0

(These standings are historic. It was the first time in eighty years that an Iowa team had finished unbeaten in Big Ten play.)

passing efficiency. For a guy who was more noted coming out of junior college for his quick feet and scrambling ability rather than an accurate right arm, it bordered on the unbelievable.

Banks, who was seldom used the year before in his first season at Iowa, made such a rapid rise to prominence that the Associated Press recognized him as the national Player of the Year. Although he didn't win the Heisman Trophy, he came close—second only to another quarterback, Carson Palmer of Southern California. It was the fourth time in history that a Hawkeye star had finished runner-up in voting for the Heisman. Tackle Alex Karras accomplished a rarity when he placed second in 1957, one of only two interior linemen ever to finish that high (Ohio State's John Hicks was the other in 1973).

Iowa's other two runners-up were All-America quarterbacks Randy Duncan in 1958 and Chuck Long in 1985, both of whom, like Banks, were extremely accurate passers. Long's second-place finish behind Auburn running back Bo Jackson was the closest vote in Heisman history.

Iowa began the 2002 season with a 3–1 record in nonconference play, losing to intrastate rival Iowa State, and Banks gave a hint of what was to come by throwing 6 touchdown passes in those games. The real sign that Hawkeye fans might be in for a special season came in the Big Ten opener at Penn State, a 42–35 overtime victory in which Banks passed for 261 yards and 4 touchdowns.

Back home the next week, it was another thriller against pass-minded Purdue. Banks had 2 more scoring passes, one when he teamed with tight end Dallas Clark for a 95-yard touchdown, and the other on a late-game toss to Clark that pulled out a 31–28 victory.

Banks was on a roll by then. He passed for 3 touchdowns in an unexpectedly easy 34–9 triumph at Michigan, a career-high 275 yards to beat Wisconsin, and a perfect 10 for 10 and 3 more touchdowns in a rout of Northwestern.

At the end of the regular season, Iowa boasted an overall 11–1 record, the best in school history, and their high-powered offense racked up an average of 37.2 points per game, a school record. It was so dominant that seven of the twelve spots on the All–Big Ten offensive team went to Iowa players.

The Hawks made a steady climb in the national polls and into the Bowl Championship Series. They went into postseason

Brad Banks, Iowa's star
quarterback in 2002,
breaks free on one of
his scrambling touch-
down runs.

Iowa's Big Ten Most Valuable Players

1929	Willis Glassgow, HB
1933	Joe Laws, QB
1939	Nile Kinnick, HB
1951	Bill Reichardt, FB
1956	Kenny Ploen, QB
1958	Randy Duncan, QB
1985	Chuck Long, QB
1990	Nick Bell, RB
2002	Brad Banks, QB

play ranked third in the polls and fifth in the BCS, where they were paired against the University of Southern California in the Orange Bowl. They didn't perform as they had during the season, however, although the Trojans had a lot to do with that. USC pulled away in the second half to win, 37–18.

The Hawkeyes wound up eighth in the polls, their highest ranking in forty-three years. They repeated that finish in 2003 with a 10–3 record, capping that off with a 37–17 romp over Florida in the Outback Bowl. Banks was gone but another junior-college transfer, Nathan Chandler, proved to be a capable successor.

The 2003 outfit produced one more national award winner, huge offensive tackle Robert Gallery, whose specialty was clearing a path for a small but elusive running back, Fred Russell. Gallery became the third Hawkeye to win the Outland Trophy as the nation's number one interior lineman. The others played in the Forest Evashevski era: Calvin Jones and Alex Karras.

Not the least of the attributes was Nate Kaeding, an All-America kicker who left after the 2003 season holding most of Iowa's placekicking records. He won the Lou Groza award as the nation's number one placekicker in 2002.

Here are five more star performers for the Iowa Hawkeyes:

Aubrey Devine

Devine may have played the greatest all-around game in Iowa history, accounting for all the points when the Hawkeyes drubbed Minnesota, 41–7, at Minneapolis in 1921. Iowa was in the midst of a school record twenty-game winning streak and this was victory number eight.

Although official records didn't start at Iowa and most other schools until the late 1930s, what Devine did that day remains unmatched in Hawkeye annals. He scored 29 points, rushing for 4 touchdowns and dropkicking 5 extra points. Since the Iowa record book doesn't go back that far, the recognized school mark is 24 points by seven players who had 4-touchdown games.

Devine threw touchdown passes of 43 and 25 yards to end Lester Belding for the other Iowa scores. His afternoon's work included 164 yards on 34 scrimmage plays, plus another 180 yards on kick returns, and he did all this despite being an obvious target.

Tait Cummins, a Cedar Rapids writer-broadcaster of yester-year, recalled the scene this way: "Given a terrific beating by the big Gophers, Aubrey played part of the game without knowing who he was or where he was, but instinct carried him along. Minnesota's fans may not have enjoyed what he did to their team that day, but they rose in a body to cheer him when he left the

Aubrey Devine, one of Iowa's first All-Americans, accounted for all 41 Hawkeye points in a 1921 game against Minnesota.

game." Dr. Henry L. Williams, Minnesota's Hall of Fame coach, heaped on the accolades as well, calling Devine "the greatest football player who ever stepped on Northrup Field."

Nile Kinnick

Kinnick's game against Indiana in 1939 probably came the closest of any Iowa player to what Devine accomplished. Some may deem it even better.

The Hawks won a high-scoring affair, 32–29, with Kinnick firing 3 touchdown passes, the last one to win the game in the closing minutes. Nile also scored once himself, but it's what he did in all phases while playing the full sixty minutes that was so astonishing. When you add everything up, they totaled 603 yards. "He did the work of what seven players would do today in the modern game," said Al Couppee, who was the quarterback on the 1939 team.

Kinnick's day went like this:

- Runs from scrimmage: 19 for 103 yards, an average of 5.4
- Passes: 4 completions for 108 yards, an average of 27.0
- Punt returns: 9 for 201 yards, an average of 22.3
- Kickoff returns: 6 for 171 yards, an average of 28.5
- Extra points: 2 dropkicks
- Pass interceptions: 1 for 20 yards
- Punts: 4 for 172 yards, an average of 43.0

"Obviously, in this day and age," said Couppee, "a Kinnick wouldn't be doing all those things. But when you look at the stats and compare them to what an average player would do today, you'd have to wonder why a Kinnick wouldn't be employed to do the same things. Well, first you'd have to find a Kinnick."

Ed Podolak

Successful seasons and bowl teams tend to overshadow a lot of other games that go into a school's football history, but a versatile player such as Podolak shouldn't get lost in the shuffle. He played in some of Iowa's leanest seasons, from 1966 to 1968, starting out as a quarterback in his sophomore year and moving to running back early in 1967.

The highlight came near the end of his senior season, in a home game against Northwestern, when he smashed through the Wildcats for 286 yards in a 68–34 rout. It was a Big Ten rushing record at the time and is still the best an Iowa runner has ever done in a conference game.

Podolak, who went on to an outstanding pro career with the Kansas City Chiefs, might have broken the Big Ten mark for total offense, except he was sidelined in the last quarter with a shoulder injury. He had also connected on 2 passes earlier in the game, giving him 320 yards in total offense, only 18 shy of the league record.

In those days Coach Ray Nagel awarded two game balls afterwards, one to an offensive player and another on defense, but there was only one honoree that afternoon—and it was done well before the game was over. Nagel gave Podolak the game ball at the end of the third quarter. "If Eddie isn't an All–Big Ten back this season," said Nagel, "then I never expect to have one at Iowa. This kid is as good an athlete as I have ever coached."

Podolak did make the All–Big Ten team, the only Iowa running back to be so honored for seventeen years from 1962–79. When his collegiate career ended, he had completed the best rushing season in Iowa history (937 yards) and owned the career

Ed Podolak (14) was a versatile Hawkeye star in the late 1960s.

record for total offense (4,026). The school's 2004 record book shows he is still twelfth in single-season rushing and seventh on the all-time list in total offense.

Chuck Long

Passing was the name of the game for Chuck Long, and when he left Iowa after a star-studded career he had amassed 10,461 yards

Rare Feat for MVP

In 1951 Iowa fullback Bill Reichardt pulled off what may have been an unmatched feat in the history of college football. He was named the Big Ten's most valuable player on a team that didn't win a conference game.

The Hawkeyes posted a 2–5–2 record that year, beating Kansas State and Pittsburgh in nonleague games, tying both Minnesota and Notre Dame, but losing the other five. Reichardt was a one-man gang, rushing for 737 yards to set an Iowa single-season record that lasted for eighteen years.

through the air in four seasons from 1982 to 1985. It was a Big Ten record that has been exceeded only once since: by Purdue's Drew Brees with 11,792 from 1997–2000.

Long's best performance came in the inaugural Freedom Bowl in Anaheim, California, when he shelled Texas with 6 touchdown passes in Iowa's 55–17 victory. The game was played on a wet field after heavy rains, and while the score seems to indicate a runaway, such was not the case. The Hawks did jump out to an early 14–0 lead, but they led by only 24–17 at halftime.

Long did most of his damage in a sensational third quarter, completing 12 of 14 passes for 241 yards and 4 touchdowns. The final score was on the board at the end of the period.

Iowa coach Hayden Fry was overjoyed afterwards, and with good reason. Fry, a native Texan, had struggled for years trying to beat Texas without success in his coaching years at Southern Methodist, and as a Baylor player before that. "Those folks

Chuck Long was the first player in the Big Ten to pass for more than 10,000 yards in a career.

down in Texas don't beat Texas very often," Fry exclaimed. "All my life I've wanted to beat them. The difference was that not many folks down South throw the football at those Texas guys the way we did."

Long spread the scoring around. Two of his touchdown passes went to Jonathon Hayes and 1 each to Mike Flagg, Bill Happel, Robert Smith, and Scott Helverson. Happel's 8 catches netted 104 yards and Smith had 4 for 115.

A Sad Ending

Fate was not kind to Oran "Nanny" Pape, a speedy Iowa halfback of the late 1920s. His main claim to fame came in two consecutive upsets of Minnesota, when he scored the touchdowns that beat the Gophers and Bronko Nagurski, 7–6 in 1928, and again the following year, 9–7.

Pape was one of the athletes caught up in the scandal that brought Iowa's suspension from the Big Ten in 1930, although his involvement turned out to be a mistake. However, he could not participate in his senior season. Pape joined the fledgling Iowa Highway Patrol and was later shot and killed in an armed robbery—the first patrol officer to die in the line of duty.

Chuck Hartlieb

Iowa's two chuckin' Chucks, Long and Hartlieb, monopolized All–Big Ten quarterback honors in the 1980s, taking that spot on all-conference teams five times in a six-year period. Long was voted the best in 1983, 1984, and 1985, and Hartlieb in 1987 and 1988.

With Hartlieb, it was almost a case of whatever you can do I can do better. Long's school records for 461 yards passing and 6 touchdown throws against Texas lasted only until Hartlieb amassed 471 yards with 7 touchdown passes in a 1987 game at Northwestern.

Hartlieb powered a Hawkeye onslaught that shattered 19 Iowa, Big Ten, and NCAA records in a 52–24 triumph. Four of his touchdown passes went to wide receiver Quinn Early, who

Chuck Hartlieb passed for 558 yards in one game and threw 7 touchdown passes in another.

had an equally glorious day with 256 yards in receptions. He combined with Hartlieb on a 95-yard scoring play that set an Iowa record for distance and also tied a conference mark.

The game was not as one-sided as it might appear because Northwestern twice led by 10 points in the first half. Then Hartlieb broke it open with 4 touchdown passes in the third quarter, also equaling what Long had done three years earlier. "Northwestern kept playing the run, so we kept passing," explained Fry, although he risked giving Hartlieb a sore arm. After throwing his seventh touchdown pass in the third quarter, Hartlieb came over to the bench and said, "Coach, let someone else play. I've had enough." Hartlieb had an even busier day the next year in a 45–34 victory at Indiana, completing 40 passes for 558 yards, both of which are school records.

A Proud Legacy

Iowans can be justly proud of their state university's rich tradition in treating black athletes with dignity and respect, permitting them to play football decades before many schools would even let African Americans attend all-white colleges, much less allow them on the playing fields. One of Iowa's first consensus All-Americans in 1921 was a brawny black tackle named Fred "Duke" Slater, who later sat on the bench as a municipal judge in Chicago. Others became engineers, teachers, coaches, mayors, and state legislators. Emlen Tunnell, leading passer for the Hawkeyes in 1946, later starred as defensive back in the National Football League, and he was the first black player inducted into the Pro Football Hall of Fame.

Iowa also was the team that ended segregation in the Orange Bowl when the 1950 Hawks took five African-American athletes to Florida for their season finale at the University of Miami. There were fears of possible trouble but the game went off without incident. To illustrate how unusual a game like that was at the time, Miami didn't admit black students for another ten years and didn't integrate its athletic teams until 1967.

Iowa's first black player was Carleton "Kinney" Holbrook, a swift running back who lettered on teams in 1895 and 1896. The 1895 outfit was a disorganized and undistinguished lot, but the following season the university hired its first paid coach, A. E. Bull from Pennsylvania, and Holbrook blossomed under his direction. He scored 12 touchdowns, several on game-winning runs, and the Hawkeye record of 7–1–1 was the best since football had its beginnings on the campus in 1889.

Like many African-American athletes to come, Holbrook's presence was not accepted in some places. One was at the University of Missouri, which threatened to call off the game in Columbia if Holbrook took the field. Coach Bull stood his ground and said there would be no game unless Holbrook could play. That set the tone for an unpleasant afternoon and according to press reports, the Iowa players came home with a sour taste for the entire proceedings.

Iowa managed to win the game, 12–0, and Holbrook scored one of the touchdowns, but it was a brutal contest with many unsportsmanlike penalties. Venom was directed at the whole Iowa team, and at one point two Missouri players slugged the referee from behind and knocked him out of the game.

The Iowa-Missouri series was discontinued for several years. When it had resumed by 1910, the Hawkeyes boasted another outstanding black player, an engineering student named Archie Alexander, a lineman who was later chosen on Iowa's all-decade team at the start of the twentieth century. Once again, early in the 1910 season, Missouri fans became riled upon learning that an African American would be playing for the Hawks.

There is a durable story that a mob of Columbia residents and students met the train bearing the Iowa team, determined not to let Alexander disembark. They were armed with pitchforks and clubs. "They needn't have worried," recalled Alexander years later, after he'd become a successful engineer helping build some of the river bridges in Des Moines. "I wasn't on the train. That was one of the big disappointments of my life. Our coach, Jess Hawley, didn't even come to me and tell me he was leaving me at home. I'd started our first two games and thought I was a regular. I didn't know I wasn't going to Columbia until I saw the traveling squad posted two days before the game. My name wasn't on it. I turned in my uniform, but the next day—after Missouri beat us, 5–0—my teammates urged me to reconsider, and I did. But I never got over that disappointment."

Hawley later revealed that Missouri officials warned him not to bring Alexander because they wouldn't allow him to play. Incensed, he told them Iowa would never again schedule Missouri as long as he was the coach, but it's been much longer than that: The two neighboring state universities have never met again in football.

They did plan a four-game series scheduled to start in 2005, but when Iowa's teams became nationally ranked in recent years, Tiger officials said they wanted to play weaker opposition and reneged on the contract for the first two games. Iowa then decided to wipe out the entire series.

Duke Slater may have been Iowa's greatest all-around lineman. Certainly he received as many plaudits as the stars who followed, making just about every All-America team in 1921. Old photos show the helmetless Slater—he was one of few players left by then who didn't wear protective headgear—blocking out four Notre Dame linemen to clear a path for Gordon Locke.

Walter Eckersall, one of the main All-America pickers of that era, said of him, "Slater is so powerful that one man can't handle him, and opposing elevens have found it necessary to send two men against him every time a play was sent off his side of the line."

Slater's reputation was long lasting, too. When Glenn "Pop" Warner selected an all-time football team in 1946, with the help of 600 sports writers nationwide, one of the tackles chosen on the starting eleven was Duke Slater. Several years later he went into the College Football Hall of Fame.

Because of the success and fame of players like Slater, word spread that Iowa was a friendly place for minority athletes at the big-time level. That's why Ozzie Simmons and his brother hopped a freight train out of Fort Worth, Texas, and wound up on the campus at Iowa City in the early 1930s. Simmons, a running back, was welcomed into the Iowa program and soon hit the headlines because of his elusive speed. Although the Hawkeyes were not especially good in that era, Simmons gave them a sparkle they'd seldom enjoyed before.

Duke Slater, who did not wear a helmet, appears to be blocking out half the Notre Dame line in this 1921 action photo.

Gradually but ever so slowly, the barriers were coming down in college sports across the country. Homer Harris, an end, became the first black captain of an Iowa football team in 1937. After World War II such top-notch athletes as Emlen Tunnell and Earl Banks signed on with the Hawks. Tunnell was more noted for his offensive play as a halfback in 1946–47, but he went on to a brilliant career as a defensive back with the New York Giants in their renowned "Umbrella Defense." His career total of 79 interceptions stood as NFL record for a number of years. Banks, a four-year letterman at guard, became a long-time coach at Morgan State and was voted into the College Football Hall of Fame.

Vincent Still Holds the Record

Eddie Vincent raced 96 yards to score in Iowa's homecoming game against Purdue on November 6, 1954, and it is still a school record for the longest touchdown run from scrimmage, and also the third longest in more than one hundred years of Big Ten football. Vincent later became prominent in California politics and was a three-term mayor of Inglewood, a Los Angeles suburb.

With Tunnell and Banks leading the way, Iowa continued to recruit promising black athletes, and the five that integrated the Orange Bowl were Bernie Bennett, Don Commack, Mike Riley, Harold Bradley, and Delmar Corbin. They gave a good account of themselves, too, because Miami had an unbeaten team in that late-November game but had to work hard for a 14–6 victory. "We were aware that we were setting a precedent," recalls Bennett, who was a sophomore halfback, "but nothing happened during the game that reflected any conflict. There was no special security and there were no racist remarks. Once the game started, we just played."

The real breakthrough for African Americans came in the fall of 1952 when new Iowa coach Forest Evashevski brought in the famed "Steubenville Trio" from Ohio: Calvin Jones, Frank Gilliam, and Eddie Vincent. They had a huge impact on Hawkeye football for years to come.

The famed Steubenville Trio that helped resurrect Iowa's football fortunes in the 1950s. From left: Frank Gilliam, Eddie Vincent, and Calvin Jones.

Jones was a powerful guard who became Iowa's first two-time consensus All-American and winner of the Outland Trophy in 1955 as the nation's outstanding lineman. Gilliam and Vincent were both All–Big Ten players. Gilliam, an end, was the team's leading pass receiver for two years, and due to an injury, he got an extra year of eligibility, playing on the winning Rose Bowl team in 1957. Vincent was Iowa's leading rusher in 1954–55.

Jones had been heavily recruited coming out of high school and was ticketed to go to Ohio State, but the Buckeyes didn't

"Thunder Foot"

One of the most valuable weapons early in the Hayden Fry era was the punting of Reggie Roby, who became known as "Thunder Foot" because of his high, booming kicks. He was one of the main reasons Iowa made it to the 1982 Rose Bowl game in Fry's third year.

Roby's name is still in the NCAA record books for having the best punting average in a season, based on a minimum of at least 40 kicks. He averaged almost half the length of the field on every attempt in 1981, totaling 2,193 yards on 44 punts for an average of 49.8 per kick.

Roby, who had a long career in pro football, died of a heart attack early in 2005. He was only forty-three.

have room for both Gilliam and Vincent. So those two decided to stick together and attend Iowa. During a summer trip in 1952 to check out the campus, Jones decided to go along and keep them company, making a minivacation out of it. Jones liked what he saw, said no to Ohio State, and the Hawkeyes had a package deal of major proportions.

There is a sad ending to the story of Calvin Jones. Spurning overtures from the NFL, Jones accepted a deal to play professionally for the Winnipeg Blue Bombers in the Canadian Football League. That was in the fall of 1956, and he was just as big a hit in the pros as he had been in college, but returning from Vancouver to Winnipeg after the Canadian all-star game, he was aboard a plane that encountered bad weather and crashed into the mountains. All sixty-two passengers aboard the commercial aircraft were killed.

When the Hawkeyes later went west for the Rose Bowl, which Jones had planned to attend, they dedicated the game to his memory. When they won they sent the game ball to his mother, Mrs. Talitha Jones.

By the mid-1950s, of course, black athletes were becoming much more commonplace, with such speedy backs as Bob Jeter, Willie Fleming, and Larry Ferguson starring in the Evashevski era. Now the top eleven career rushers are all from the ranks of African American players, topped by Sedrick Shaw, the only one to run for more than 4,000 yards (4,156 from 1993–96). It's been almost forty years since a white running back left school holding the career rushing record: Ed Podolak in 1968.

Linebacker Larry Station not only joined Calvin Jones as Iowa's only other two-time consensus All-American in 1984–1985, he was an Academic All-American as well. Defensive ends Andre Tippett and Leroy Smith both earned consensus All-America honors in the Hayden Fry era, and so did Reggie Roby, one of the greatest punters ever in college football.

Now teams throughout the country are filled with talented black players. Racial prejudice hasn't disappeared, of course, but it's no longer much of a factor in college athletics. There have been enormous strides since the days of Kinney Holbrook and Archie Alexander.

Memorable Moments

In Iowa lore two plays have been known for many years as "The Kick" and "The Catch." Just mention them by name and faithful followers of the Black and Gold will know immediately what you're talking about. Now there is a third. I'll call it "The Bomb." It has to be the most shocking play in Hawkeye history, a 56-yard touchdown pass from Drew Tate to Warren Holloway as time expired to give Iowa an incredible 30–25 victory over Louisiana State in the Capital One Bowl at Orlando, Florida, on January 1, 2005.

This was no Hail Mary pass, either. LSU made a critical mistake in its coverage, and Holloway took advantage of it by sprinting downfield into the clear. In the split second that Tate needed to find an open receiver, he spotted his man, but could he hit the target? From the press box it looked as though the high spiral might be too long, and that was Tate's first reaction, too. "I was scared I overthrew him," the quarterback admitted. "But once Warren caught the ball, I knew he wasn't going down."

Rarely has there been such sudden euphoria in the annals of Iowa football, which span 115 years. About 30,000 Hawkeye fans in the sellout crowd of 70,229 went wild with joy, some screaming, others jumping up and down, high-fiving each other, some even crying. Since the game was on ABC-TV leading into the Rose Bowl, countless thousands more Iowa followers nationwide were able to see The Bomb and join in the celebration at home.

What made the play seem even more unreal was that LSU had battled back from a 24–12 deficit in the fourth quarter to take a 25–24 lead with 46 seconds remaining. Iowa fans were almost resigned to the fact that their team had played well but it wasn't quite good enough.

"We were playing for a field goal at the end," said Iowa coach Kirk Ferentz about his last-minute strategy. But with the Hawks unable to get across midfield and with precious seconds ticking away when they failed to use one of their two remaining time-outs, it came down to one last chance—a play called "All Up." The ball was on Iowa's 44 yard line with the clock showing :07 seconds left, then :06 as Tate faded to pass. Wide receiver Ed Hinkel ran down the right side, tight end Scott Chandler took off

A joyous Warren Holloway (86) is held aloft by teammates after Iowa's amazing 30–25 victory over LSU in the 2005 Capital One Bowl.

down the middle but on the same side as Hinkel, and Holloway split them.

Two things made the play work: First, not calling a time-out actually was a lucky break because LSU did not have time to set up a defense, leading to a miscommunication. Cornerback Ronnie

Let's Hear It for the Defense

Like most coaches, Hayden Fry looks beyond the obvious when he talks of big plays. Rob Houghtlin's field goal to defeat Michigan in 1985 will never be forgotten by those who saw it, but Fry remembers something of equal importance that made the kick possible.

"Michigan had a third-and-one situation late in the game," Fry recalled. "If they made it they probably would have run out the clock. They gave the ball to their tough running back (Jamie Morris), and Larry Station came out of nowhere to throw him for a three-yard loss. We didn't have a stunt on or anything like that. Larry just made the play on his own." Michigan was forced to punt and the Hawks launched their drive to set up Houghtlin's climactic three-pointer.

George Wine, Iowa's sports information director emeritus, added an interesting slant on Station's key tackle. "After the game, Morris was asked what happened on that play," said Wine, "and he said when Michigan came out of the huddle, he glanced across the line of scrimmage and Station was staring him right in the eye. He said he thought about calling time-out to change the play, but fortunately for us he didn't do it."

Prude thought the Tigers were in zone coverage instead of man-to-man, so he mistakenly left Holloway uncovered. And second, LSU did not put on a strong rush, giving Tate time to scan the field.

Holloway caught the pass in full stride at the 16 yard line, shook off a leaping defensive back who had been guarding Hinkel, and sprinted into the end zone. It was the first and only touchdown of his college career.

In the pandemonium that followed, with the scoreboard clock showing 0:00, Holloway was almost smothered as jubilant teammates engulfed him in a mass of humanity. When he escaped that, they hoisted him onto their shoulders and he waved his helmet in a joyous victory salute. Later he said, "This is like a

Down Go the Goal Posts

Iowa's last game of the regular season in 1982 included an odd and amusing incident probably without parallel in Hawkeye history. A player knocked down the goal posts, not some happy fans.

The Hawks were winding up at Michigan State, which had not won a home game all year. It was a tradition in East Lansing for the students to tear down the goal posts if the Spartans won their last game. Rather than risk losing a pair of expensive uprights, Michigan State officials took down the permanent posts and replaced them with lightweight wooden ones—not exactly balsa wood but close to it. "They must have been expecting to beat us," quipped Hayden Fry.

In the second quarter Iowa's Ron Hawley was running across the back of the end zone on pass defense when he collided with the lightweight wood. As Michigan State's pass attempt sailed harmlessly out of the end zone, it was a comical scene: Hawley fell to the ground as the posts teetered for a second and then toppled over. Hawley wasn't hurt, of course, and workers quickly put the temporary posts back in place so the Spartans could try a field goal. They made the kick but Iowa won the game.

Two Long Touchdown Runs

Two of the longest touchdown runs in the annals of Iowa football came in the same half of a home game against Oregon in 1949. The Hawks trailed late in the third quarter, 24–6, before launching the biggest comeback in school history to win, 34–31.

Bob Longley started the rally with a 94-yard punt return, which has been topped only once, a 95-yard runback by Billy Happel at Minnesota in 1984. Bill Reichardt later returned an Oregon kickoff 99 yards, the fourth best ever by an Iowa player.

dream. It's my first touchdown—ever—and we win the game against LSU in a bowl. You can't write a better script than that."

There have been many other dramatic moments in Iowa's football past, of course, but only a few to win big games in the closing seconds. In Iowa's famed 7–6 upset of Notre Dame in 1939, Nile Kinnick's touchdown plunge came in the second quarter. When the Hawks earned their first Rose Bowl bid with a 6–0 victory over Ohio State in 1956, the scoring pass from Ken Ploen to Jim Gibbons was in the third period. Both The Kick and The Catch were late-game heroics that produced spectacular endings. One beat Michigan, the other beat Ohio State, and that's enough right there to burn them into the memory bank forever.

When Iowa played Michigan in Iowa City on October 19, 1985, it was a rare regular-season matchup of teams ranked first

Rob Houghtlin kicks the last-second field goal that gave Iowa a 12-10 victory over Michigan in 1985. University of Iowa Photo Service

and second in the country. The clash of titans lived up to its billing. Both teams had great difficulty scoring, so tough were the defenses, and number one Iowa finally escaped with a 12–10 victory when Rob Houghtlin kicked a 29-yard field goal on the last play of the game.

That touched off probably the wildest celebration in the long history of Kinnick Stadium. The game ended at dusk under portable lights, because there had been a mid-afternoon kickoff to accommodate national TV, and fans stormed the field to tear down the steel goal posts. They milled around for what seemed like hours, relishing the outcome and not wanting to leave.

Houghtlin became known for making clutch kicks. He kicked a field goal after time had expired to beat Minnesota, 30–27, in the final game of the 1986 regular season, and then in the Holiday Bowl that followed he booted a 41-yarder on the final play to sink San Diego State, 39–38.

Two years after The Kick toppled Michigan came The Catch, but there would be no similar celebration. That one happened on foreign turf, leaving a sellout throng of 90,000 in Ohio State's famed horseshoe sitting in stunned disbelief at what had just occurred. Facing a seemingly impossible situation, trailing 27–22, fourth down, and 23 yards to go on Ohio State's 28 with only seconds remaining, Hawkeye quarterback Chuck Hartlieb teamed with tight end Marv Cook for a touchdown pass that let Iowa win, 29–27.

Cook caught the ball about 10 yards out and only his strength and sheer determination carried him over the goal line. Two Buckeye defenders were hanging on his back and one of them, Bo Pellini, has insisted for years that it shouldn't have been a touchdown, claiming Cook never reached the end zone. The officials ruled otherwise.

Up in the broadcast booth, Jim Zabel, veteran sportscaster for WHO in Des Moines, screamed into his microphone, "I love it, I love it, I love it!" and was kissed by his overjoyed broadcast partner, Eddie Podolak. "I've broadcast hundreds of football games in over fifty years, most of them Iowa games, and that tops my list of all-time great plays," said Zabel. "The fact that it happened at Ohio State made it all the more incredible."

Donnie Patterson, head coach at Western Illinois, said he'll remember that play as long as he lives. He was Hayden Fry's offensive coordinator at the time. "Coach Fry called 'Y Trail,'

Marv Cook clutches the ball after scoring the winning touchdown against Ohio State in 1987. © 1987 Cedar Rapids Gazette/Paul Jensen

which was a pass to Cook down the right side," Patterson said. "Marv caught the ball on the 10 yard line, spun away from one defensive back, and then carried two others the last 3 yards into the end zone. Up to that time I'd been coaching Iowa's tight ends for eight years," he added, "and I told Marv afterwards that he played the best game by a tight end that I'd ever seen."

It was this loss, incidentally, that cost beleaguered Ohio State coach Earle Bruce his job, even though he had compiled the best record among Big Ten coaches in his nine years at Columbus. The following Saturday Bruce got a measure of personal revenge when his team upset Michigan.

An Explosion in the Radio Booth

Gary Dolphin, voice of the Hawkeyes, became so excited as he described The Bomb to the radio audience back home that he was hoarse for days after the Capital One Bowl game. This is how he called the closing seconds:

"Here's Tate . . . They wind the clock. Drew's gotta go . . . 30 seconds to play. Tate wants to throw left but comes over the middle instead. Got him. Is it a catch? Sure looks like it, but it's not enough for a first down. They've gotta call time-out. Call time-out, Drew. Fifteen seconds to go. Now he spikes the ball. [Iowa was penalized 5 yards for illegal procedure and then the clock was restarted.]

"They wind the clock. They've gotta call time-out. Nine seconds to play but Drew Tate doesn't know that. The game's gonna end on this play. He fires downfield . . . It's caught . . . And into the end zone! TOUCHDOWN IOWA, TOUCHDOWN IOWA! No time on the clock. I don't believe what I just saw. TOUCH-DOWN IOWA! Oh, my God, I can't believe what I just saw!

"Was it Solomon? No, it was Holloway, the forgotten man, the forgotten man. Drew Tate tried to hand the game to LSU, he wouldn't call time-out. He didn't know the clock had started and he just fired a touchdown pass of 60 yards [it was 56]. Oh, my goodness. LSU cheated to the outside and Holloway ran right by the safety. I didn't think he was going to get in. I thought he was going to get tackled at the 10.

"Unbelievable. Incredible. I cannot describe what we just saw. We just went to the Land of Oz."

Several longtime media members were asked to discount the obvious choices and pinpoint other highlight plays from the past. Cedar Rapids broadcaster Bob Brooks, who probably has seen more Iowa games than anyone during his sixty-year career, goes all the way back to the 1956 Ohio State game, describing the pass from Kenny Ploen to Jim Gibbons that sent Iowa to the Rose Bowl. "That was the defining moment of the Forest Evashevski era at Iowa," Brooks said. "Ohio State had a long Big Ten winning streak at the time, and that game legitimized Iowa as one of the top teams in the country."

The late Al Grady of Iowa City, who covered the Hawkeyes longer than any other sportswriter, used to say one of his favorite moments was an unusual play that most longtime fans had forgotten about. It led to an amazing turnabout, a 67-yard touchdown run with a midair fumble recovery by Joe Williams in 1960 that rescued the Hawks at Michigan State. "Then Bernie Wyatt intercepted a Michigan State pass," explained Grady, "and Wilburn Hollis scored on a quarterback sneak when he was just trying to run out the clock. Instead of what seemed to be a certain defeat, Iowa won, 27–15."

That victory was important in keeping what may have been Forest Evashevski's best team in the running for the national championship. Only a late loss to Minnesota denied the Hawks of that prize, and they had to settle for number two in the final UPI poll, number three in the AP poll.

Another nail-biter against Michigan State, this one in 1985 in Kinnick Stadium, was also crucial in the national polls when Iowa was number one for five straight weeks. That game's thrilling finish was a favorite of Ron Gonder, longtime Cedar Rapids sportscaster. "Time was running out on the Hawks and

A 102-Yard Punt

Although Iowa's 1934 game at Indiana was a scoreless tie played on a wet field, it earned a place in history for one reason. Standing in his own end zone, Hawkeye punter Dick Crayne boomed a kick that traveled more than 90 yards past the scrimmage line, rolling out of bounds on the Indiana 5 yard line. The distance from Crayne's foot: 102 yards!

they were behind, 31–28," Gonder said. "They had the ball on Michigan State's 1 yard line but it was fourth down—one more play to win or lose. There were no overtimes then and Iowa wasn't playing for a tie. Hayden Fry called time-out to discuss the situation with Chuck Long. He told Long to go back into the huddle and call a line plunge to Ronnie Harmon—but not to give the ball to Harmon. Instead, he was to keep the ball and take it on a bootleg around right end.

"Well, it worked to perfection. There was a massive pileup at the line of scrimmage—even all the Iowa players thought Harmon had the ball—and Chuck raced around the end all alone. Before he got to the goal line, he was waving the ball in the air. I don't think Hayden was too happy about that." It wasn't a risky maneuver, though, because nobody was near Long, and a 35–31 victory was safely in the books.

Many plays don't produce game-winning scores but they are crucial to the outcome. One such fourth-quarter play helped

Iowa save a 14–13 victory at home against Illinois in 1982, when both teams were in title contention and battling for a high finish in the Big Ten. Iowa was stuck in a third-and-29 situation deep in its own territory in the closing minutes. If the Hawks were forced to punt, Illinois would get the ball in good field position for its ace kicker, with a strong wind at his back. He'd already made 2 field goals. The Illini didn't get the chance, however, because Eddie Phillips ran 30 yards on a draw play and the game was all but over.

Scroll ahead twenty years to what Iowa faced at its homecoming game in 2002, trailing Purdue 28–24 with 2:16 remaining, first down for the Hawks on their 13 yard line. Only a quarterback with the shifty feet of Brad Banks could have done what he did, scrambling into the open and darting 44 yards past midfield. A little later Banks lofted the winning touchdown pass to tight end Dallas Clark.

Former Hawkeye athletic director Bump Elliott's favorite play was the very first to begin the Fry era in 1979. It was against Indiana. The Hawks lined up in a spread offense with no running backs, and Phil Suess fired a 10-yard pass completion over the middle. "Iowa fans weren't used to seeing anything like that," Elliott said. "They all stood up and cheered, and to me that signaled the start of a new era in Iowa football."

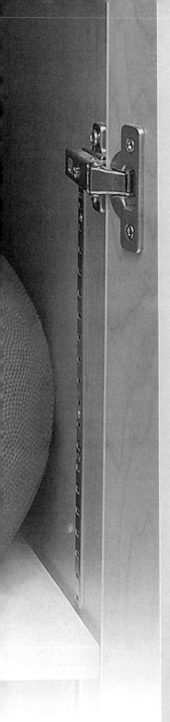

Big Upsets of the Big Ten's Big Two

There is no clearer illustration of how Michigan and Ohio State have dominated the Big Ten than to count their combined number of football championships. In a little more than a hundred years of conference play, those two have won or shared 70 titles: 41 by Michigan and 29 by Ohio State. It's easy to understand why victories over these two teams are so cherished, especially when you go for many years without being able to beat either one. During one period Iowa lost sixteen straight times to Ohio State. And in a

Deep Six'd

In 1981 there was something weird about being ranked sixth in the country. Iowa upset number six Nebraska in the season opener, and when UCLA visited Iowa City two weeks later, the Bruins came in also ranked number six, only to go down in defeat.

Those victories moved the Hawkeyes into the national rankings for the first time in many years. Then they stunned a Michigan team that also happened to be ranked sixth in the polls. So guess which team became the new number six the following week? Yep, Iowa. Bad news. The Hawks were immediately knocked off their unlucky perch by Minnesota, 12–10.

mid-century stretch of fifty-five years, the Hawkeyes managed to top Michigan only twice in twenty-seven tries.

The more you lose, the easier it is to accept. That's what faced Forest Evashevski in the 1950s and Hayden Fry some thirty years later, when they were hired to resurrect losing programs at Iowa. To play with the big boys, you had to be able to beat them once in a while.

Evashevski did it almost immediately, taking over a ragtag Iowa team in 1952 and scoring one of the most shocking upsets in Big Ten history, knocking off Ohio State in his first season, 8–0. One of Fry's biggest victories came in his third year, a stunning 9–7 victory at Michigan in 1981, setting the tone for his many successes that followed. Here are some reflections on those games from two players who had key roles in what transpired.

Iowa 8, Ohio State 0

The date was October 25, 1952. It was homecoming in Iowa City but there didn't figure to be much to celebrate. Iowa had lost its first four games that season and the opponent, Ohio State, had routed the Hawks by scores of 83–21 and 47–21 in the two previous years.

Evashevski would be matching wits for the first time with Woody Hayes, who was in his second year with the Buckeyes and on his way to becoming a coaching legend. The two men would stage some great battles in the next few years, but Hayes seemed to be holding all the cards for this one.

Burt Britzmann (pronounced BRIGHTS-man) was the Iowa quarterback that day. He recalled the practices leading up to the game as "the worst week of my life," because Evashevski suddenly decided on a new plan of attack. "Evy changed our whole offense the week of the game," Britzmann explained. "We went from a wing-T formation to a spread formation. The linemen were split a yard or a yard and a half apart, which spread out the defense. But the biggest change for me was that all the plays were called from the line of scrimmage. We'd always used a huddle before, so this took a lot of getting used to—especially for me.

"There was one quote from Evy that I'll never forget. We were having a hard time in practice and he was like an emperor, sitting up in the stands watching us. At one point he yelled down, 'Britzmann, you jackass, get out of there.'"

When kickoff time arrived before a crowd of 44,659, the Hawks were ready to spring their surprise. Evashevski knew they didn't have the speed to do much damage on the outside against the faster Ohio State defenders, and he hoped the strategy of

Coach Forest Evashevski speaks via telephone to his assistants in the press box during a game in the 1950s.

splitting the linemen would create some holes on the inside. "The first series Ohio State was really confused," Britzmann said with a chuckle. "I remember the linebackers looking over at Woody and spreading their arms, like, 'What do we do?' and I think he was confused for a while, too."

With the Iowa offense enjoying modest success, much more than expected, the defensive unit joined in with an inspired performance that throttled Ohio State's every move. The Buckeyes rushed for only 42 yards and never got past the Iowa 28 yard line all afternoon.

"The Hawks walked with the gods Saturday," Bill Bryson wrote in the *Des Moines Register*. "They played the heralded Buckeyes off their feet. The aggressive, savage tackling gave them a safety in the second quarter. They could have made that skimpy lead stand up, so relentless were their charges and countercharges, but they added insurance to their trembling advantage by scoring a fourth-quarter touchdown that grew from Bernie Bennett's amazing 44-yard punt return to Ohio State's 25 yard line."

Britzmann started the short scoring drive with a 2-yard run, but he wasn't around to see the clinching touchdown, which came on Binkey Broeder's fourth-down plunge from the 1 foot line. Burt made a diving catch of Bobby Stearnes's left-handed pass at the 19, and when he landed he suffered a shoulder separation—his throwing shoulder. Jackie Hess replaced him. "I played the rest of the season but didn't throw much in practice," said Britzmann. "I needed pain-killers to make it through the games."

That was the last season of platoon football, with rules limiting substitutions (players had to go both ways) prevailing for the next ten years, and most of the postgame plaudits went to the aroused Hawkeye defenders. They made life miserable for Ohio State quarterback John Borton, who was smeared for losses totaling 42 yards. Borton's 37 pass attempts were one shy of the Big Ten record.

The Buckeyes had won three of their first four games that year and went on to post a 5–2 record in Big Ten play, finishing third. The startling loss to Iowa eventually cost them the conference title and sent Wisconsin to the Rose Bowl. Evashevski's Hawks won only one other game, routing Northwestern, 39–14, and they wound up with a record of 2–7. The Ohio State upset was definitely a sign of things to come.

"What he did in changing our offense that week was just the beginning of Evy's offensive genius," said Britzmann, who later became a doctor and had a family practice for many years in

Iowa's Top 10 Football Games

Iowa's top ten games, listed here in order of importance, are:

1. 2005 Capital One Bowl: Drew Tate threw a 56-yard touchdown pass to Warren Holloway on the last play of the game, giving the Hawks a stunning 30–25 victory over LSU. Tate was voted the game's MVP.

2. 1959 Rose Bowl: After beating California, 38–12, Iowa was voted the nation's number one team by the Football Writers Association of America. Bob Jeter rushed for 194 yards on just 9 carries, including an 81-yard touchdown run, and won MVP honors.

3. 1985 vs. Michigan: This was a rare regular-season matchup of the nation's top two teams. Rob Houghtlin's 4 field goals, the last as time expired, let number one Iowa edge number two Michigan, 12–10.

4. 1957 Rose Bowl: Iowa's first trip to a bowl game was a happy one, a 35–19 victory over Oregon State. Hawkeye quarterback Kenny Ploen was the MVP, hitting 9 of 10 passes and scoring on a 49-yard run.

5. 1939 vs. Notre Dame: Nile Kinnick's second-quarter touchdown and dropkick for the extra point gave Iowa a 7–6 victory and one of the greatest upsets in school history.

6. 2004 Outback Bowl: The Hawks finished number eight in the national polls for the second straight year by beating Florida, 37-17. Fred Russell rushed for 150 yards and a touchdown to win the MVP award.

7. 1921 vs. Notre Dame: This was a shocker of an earlier era, a 10-7 Hawkeye victory that was Notre Dame's only loss in forty games spread over five seasons. Gordon Locke's touchdown plunge and Aubrey Devine's 38-yard dropkick for a field goal produced the Iowa points.

8. 1956 vs. Ohio State: Iowa clinched the Big Ten title and its first Rose Bowl trip with a tense 6-0 victory. End Jim Gibbons scored the touchdown on a 17-yard pass from Kenny Ploen in the third quarter. The shutout was Iowa's fourth of the season.

9. 1939 vs. Minnesota: The Hawks had not beaten old nemesis Minnesota in ten years, but Nile Kinnick dipped into his bag of tricks one more time, throwing touchdown passes to Erwin Prasse and Bill Green in the last quarter to pull out a 13-9 victory.

10. 1981 at Michigan: Tom Nichol's 3 field goals and a stout defense let Iowa defeat the Wolverines for the first time in twenty years, 9-7, a key victory in the surprising Hawkeye march to the Rose Bowl.

Moscow, Idaho. "One other thing I remember about that game was what happened as soon as it was over. The guys picked up Evy to carry him off the field, and I grabbed his hat and put it on. I still have a picture of that."

It was quite a climax to Britzmann's "hell week." The jackass and his teammates had come through.

Iowa 9, Michigan 7

Tom Nichol remembers more about what happened after the game at Ann Arbor in 1981 than he does any of his three field goals that furnished all the Iowa points. Coach Hayden Fry presented him with the game ball, heady stuff for a freshman not too long out of high school in Green Bay, Wisconsin.

"It was such an incredible feeling," Nichol remembered. "When we got to the locker room after the game, the guys were all pumped up and we started singing 'Who's afraid of the big bad wolf, the big bad wolf, the big bad wolf? Not Iowa!' Then Coach Fry came in, the place quieted down, there was a prayer, and then he said, 'The game ball goes to Tommy Nichol.' I was shocked. We were a defensive team, the defense had won the game, and for me to be singled out was quite an honor. Later I had all the guys sign it. I treasure that ball."

Hawkeye fans treasured the victory. It was only the fifth for Iowa in the long Michigan series, which started in 1900, and it certainly ranks among the most important of the Fry era, being instrumental in a Big Ten co-championship and Rose Bowl trip.

Earlier in the season the Hawks had knocked off two nationally ranked powers in Iowa City—Nebraska and UCLA—to signal their arrival as a team to be reckoned with in Fry's third year as coach. But there were two key injuries in the UCLA game that would cause some changes in Iowa's lineup, one of which brought Nichol to the forefront. Lon Olejniczak, the team's starting wingback and regular placekicker, was lost for the season with a broken leg. Quarterback Pete Gales went out with an abdominal injury, and Gordy Bohannon, a junior college transfer, took over and did most of the signal calling for the rest of the year.

Shortly after Olejniczak was carried from the field in the third quarter, an Iowa scoring bid was stymied in UCLA territory to set up a 50-yard field goal situation. Ordinarily, that was in Nichol's range, but when you take into account freshman jitters, there was no telling what might happen. "Coach Fry called me over and said, 'Do you think you can make that, Tommy?'" Nichol recalled. "I was so nervous I thought I might get sick, but of course I said, 'Sure, I can make it.'

"When I trotted out onto the field, I remember thinking, 'Just get it airborne, just get it airborne.' I got off a pretty good kick, actually. It just missed, and when I came off I didn't know whether to be happy or sad."

Nichol did make 2 field goals that day in Iowa's 20–7 upset of the Bruins, and the following week he tied what was then a school record with eight successful conversion kicks when the Hawks routed Northwestern, 64–0. So his nervousness was pretty much gone before the trip to Ann Arbor, even though he was a rookie kicking before a crowd of 105,000.

"You know, it's amazing how quickly you can get acclimated to a situation, whether it's in sports or a job or whatever," Nichol said. "I'd been kicking all my life. It was my passion. As a kid growing up in Green Bay, I'd be out in the snowdrifts kicking over the telephone wires. I'd go to Packer games and hang on the fence, waiting for players to give me a chinstrap. Those guys were like gods to me. Anyway, when we went to Michigan I wasn't really nervous about playing before such a big crowd. I was the kicker. That was my job. I expected to make field goals."

There had been a switch in the Iowa kicking lineup, however. Bohannon had been the holder for Olejniczak and then Nichol, but after he'd replaced Gales it was decided that rather than have him risk an injury on the placekicking tries, the job should go to somebody else—reserve quarterback Tom Grogan. "Coach Fry played that down, saying it wouldn't make any difference and it didn't," said Nichol, who made all three of his attempts that day from 20, 36, and 30 yards. The first two gave Iowa a 6–0 lead before a Michigan touchdown pass to All-American Anthony Carter put the Wolverines ahead at halftime.

With the Hawkeye defenders playing so well, Nichol added his decisive field goal in the third quarter and Iowa held on for its first victory in Michigan in more than twenty years. It was also the first time in forty-two years that Iowa won a game without scoring a touchdown.

What Is a Hawkeye?

The Hawkeye nickname dates back to territorial days, before Iowa became a state in 1846. It was taken from a name the Indians gave to Natty Bumpoo, a white scout, in James Fenimore Cooper's 1826 novel *The Last of the Mohicans.* Citizens in the Iowa Territory began referring to themselves as Hawkeyes. The Territorial Legislature made the nickname official, as did the state and eventually the University of Iowa. A hawk was depicted on the great seal of the Territory of Iowa.

Two Burlington men, Judge David Rorer and James G. Edwards, were credited with popularizing the nickname. Edwards called his newspaper the *Burlington Hawk-Eye.* It is now named *The Hawk Eye* and is Iowa's oldest newspaper.

"Admittedly, there is a certain aura about the Michigan tradition and playing in that big stadium." Nichol said. "But I remember before the first game of my freshman year when we played Nebraska. There were pictures of Nebraska players on our bulletin board along with a quote that said, REMEMBER YOU PLAY YOUR OPPONENTS, NOT THEIR REPUTATION. I think that's how we felt going to Michigan."

Nichol became one of the most accurate kickers in Iowa history in an era when Iowa did a lot of scoring, and he went to bowl games in each of his four years. He also made 142 of 147 extra-point kicks, a school record at the time. Nichol now makes his home in Appleton, Wisconsin, near Green Bay, where he and his brother are co-owners of a tool and machine shop.

The Floyd of Rosedale Story

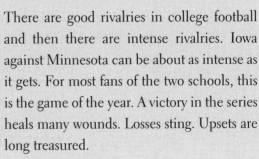

There are good rivalries in college football and then there are intense rivalries. Iowa against Minnesota can be about as intense as it gets. For most fans of the two schools, this is the game of the year. A victory in the series heals many wounds. Losses sting. Upsets are long treasured.

Minnesota is Iowa's oldest rival, dating from the first meeting in 1891, but in the beginning it was a border rivalry in name only. The Gophers to the north won every game for many years and by such lopsided scores as 34–0, 75–0, 39–0, and 41–0.

It became an achievement for Iowa just to get some points on the scoreboard. In 1912, for example, after Minnesota had posted six straight shutouts, the Hawks averted still another one when Willis O'Brien dropkicked two field goals from 50 and 51 yards in a 24–6 loss.

Finally, during the successful reign of coach Howard Jones, Iowa managed to break through by winning a 6–0 defensive struggle in 1918. That ended Minnesota's twelve-game winning streak in the series over a twenty-seven-year period and touched off a weeklong celebration in Iowa City. Iowa also won the next four meetings and the border battles became a real rivalry.

In the early 1930s Minnesota regained the upper hand and became a national power under the leadership of Bernie Bierman. Iowa, meanwhile, was shaking off the effects of a suspension from the Big Ten, but by 1934 it appeared that things were looking up for the Hawks, with the addition of a swift sophomore halfback named Ozzie Simmons.

In an early-season game against Northwestern, the elusive Simmons scored 2 touchdowns and ran for almost 200 yards in a 20–7 Hawkeye victory. Midwestern sportswriters began referring to him as the "Ebony Eel," since back in those days they felt star athletes had to have some sort of descriptive nickname. Coming up to the Minnesota game, the *Minneapolis Tribune* gave this capsule assessment of the new Iowa star: "Simmons, Negro sophomore, runs like a deer and has the knack of fading away from tacklers in a ghostlike manner that is said to be uncanny."

Ozzie Simmons was known as the "Ebony Eel" because of his shifty moves.

So the scouting report was obvious for the Gophers before they invaded Iowa City: Stop Simmons and you stop Iowa. Not only did they stop him, they punished him as well, although most of Minnesota's rough tactics went unpenalized. Ozzie, who played safety on defense, took just as much of a physical pounding while trying to tackle the bigger Gopher backs as he did when he carried the ball.

"What they were doing, what it amounted to, was that they were piling on—late hits," said Simmons in an interview many years later, after he'd retired as a Chicago schoolteacher. "Some of them should have been called, no question about it. I had bruised ribs. They did a good job on me. They came at me with knees high, and some of it was pretty obvious."

Minnesota rolled to a 34–0 halftime lead and won easily, 48–12, on its way to the national championship. Needless to say, Ozzie didn't gain much of anything that day, except maybe a bad headache. He was injured and on the sidelines long before the game was over.

Hard feelings festered for a year until the teams faced off again the following November, also in Iowa City. Both were unbeaten, the Hawkeyes having won four games and tied one, and Minnesota 5–0. Simmons was an All-America candidate by then. In the fourth game of the 1934 season he had reached a new peak when the Hawks blanked Illinois, 19–0, rushing for 192 yards, returning two kickoffs for 54 yards, running back three punts for 33 yards, and scoring 1 touchdown.

Bierman's Gophers came to town riding a 21-game unbeaten streak, and because the rivalry had become so heated, Iowa athletic officials naturally were worried about crowd control in such a highly charged atmosphere. The day before the game, Iowa governor Clyde L. Herring issued a surprising statement that only added fuel to the fire. "The University of Iowa football team will defeat the University of Minnesota tomorrow," Herring predicted. "Those Minnesotans will find ten other top-notch football players besides 'Oze' Simmons against them this year. Moreover, if the officials stand for any rough tactics like Minnesota used last year, I'm sure the crowd won't."

The message couldn't have been any plainer. "What he was saying was, 'If you treat Ozzie like you treated him last year, we're coming out of the stands,'" Simmons said.

Scouting Tips Pay Off

Back in the days when college teams personally scouted opponents, before game films and videotape made that unnecessary, Iowa discovered some valuable clues on how to thwart a Minnesota All-American who had been almost unstoppable. In mid-November of 1953 Minnesota brought a triple-threat half-back named Paul Giel to Iowa for the annual Floyd of Rosedale game. As a junior the year before, Giel was voted the Big Ten's most valuable player. Through his first two seasons he had played in 18 games, rushed or passed the ball in 577 plays, totaled 2,771 yards, and scored 18 touchdowns.

There was no letup in his senior season, either, when he ran and passed for 1,339 yards in 291 plays, becoming the Big Ten's first two-time MVP. As an example of how difficult he was to corral, in one 1953 game against Michigan, Giel handled the ball 53 times and piled up 371 all-purpose yards.

Whitey Piro, one of Forest Evashevski's assistants, scouted many of Giel's games and began to see some telltale signs of vulnerability. "He had certain mannerisms about the things he did," Piro related. "I noticed that if he kept his feet close together while he was calling the signals, that meant he planned to run up the middle, and if he spread them apart he was going to run wide. But the big thing I saw was that when he took the center snap and did start to run wide, if he raised the ball as if to pass, that meant he was going to run. If he didn't raise the ball and fake a pass, that meant he was going to pass."

Armed with that knowledge, Iowa's defenders totally frustrated Giel. He carried the ball 14 times and netted 13 yards. He completed 5 of 10 passes for only 22 yards and had 2 intercepted. Dusty Rice scored 3 touchdowns in leading Iowa to a 27–0 victory, but the unsung hero that day was Whitey Piro.

Ozzie Simmons was one of Iowa's best running backs in the 1930s.

Bierman quickly demanded that Iowa officials afford him and his players added police protection. Herring tried to calm the explosive controversy that was partly his fault by issuing another statement, saying, "A Minnesota team or any other team has nothing to fear from an Iowa audience."

Enter Minnesota governor Floyd B. Olson, who sent the following telegram to Herring, injecting some humor while attempting to defuse the troublesome situation: "Minnesota folks

A Long Career

Jerry Niles had an unusual football career at Iowa, winning his only two letters seven years apart. In 1938 he was the leading rusher on a team that won only one game. After a lengthy interruption due to World War II, he returned in 1945 and this time was the leading passer on a team that managed only one Big Ten victory. But it was a big one— over Minnesota to take back the Floyd of Rosedale trophy.

Niles rallied the Hawkeyes from a 19–6 deficit, teaming with Nelson Smith on a 50-yard screen pass for the touchdown that won the game in the closing minutes, 20–19.

excited over your statement about the Iowa crowd lynching the Minnesota football team. I have assured them that you are a law-abiding gentleman and you are only trying to get our goat. The Minnesota team will tackle clean, but, oh, how hard, Clyde. If you seriously think Iowa has any chance to win, I will bet you a Minnesota prize hog against an Iowa prize hog that Minnesota wins today. The loser must deliver the hog to the winner in person. You are getting odds because Minnesota raises better hogs than Iowa."

Herring accepted the offer, probably not because he really expected to win it, but as a way to dig himself out of a hole, and fortunately for all parties nothing untoward happened during the game. Minnesota continued its winning ways but got a fierce struggle from Simmons and the Hawkeyes before escaping with a 13–6 victory.

High-Level Gambling

The day that Iowa governor Clyde Herring marched a prize hog into the Minnesota governor's office in 1935 to pay off a football wager, he learned that an Iowa fan had sworn out a warrant charging him with illegal gambling. Minnesota governor Floyd Olson kiddingly offered asylum, but Herring declined, saying, "I might have to go home and pardon myself."

When it was over, in a scene nobody could have expected, Minnesota's players treated Simmons like a long-lost friend. They lauded him for playing a great game, causing the *Minneapolis Star* to comment, "Never have we heard so much praise for one player by the opponent in a football game as was the case with Simmons."

Carrying out his part of the bargain, Governor Herring ordered a prize pig from the Rosedale Farm near Fort Dodge, naming him Floyd of Rosedale in honor of the Minnesota governor, and personally walked him into Governor Olson's carpeted office in St. Paul. Olson donated the hog to the University of Minnesota, which commissioned a sculptor to capture Floyd's image in a permanent statue. The result is a bronze pig 21 inches long, 15½ inches high, and weighing 94 pounds.

Counting the 1935 meeting, Minnesota won nine of the first ten games in the Floyd series, with only Nile Kinnick's late-game heroics in 1939 getting Iowa into the victory column. The

The Floyd of Rosedale Trophy.

Hawkeyes have won five in a row on two different occasions, once under Forest Evashevski and again under Hayden Fry, but it was Minnesota that came out on top when the two teams met with the national championship on the line in 1960.

From the Iowa standpoint, here are five games that warmed the hearts of Hawkeye fans, one for each of the last five decades:

1956: Iowa 7, Minnesota 0

This game between two Big Ten title contenders proved to be a crucial victory for the Hawks in their drive to the school's first Rose Bowl appearance. They scored a touchdown in the first five minutes at Minnesota and that's all they needed, with their frenzied defense forcing the Gophers to turn the ball over six times.

1968: Iowa 35, Minnesota 28

Larry Lawrence scored 4 touchdowns as the underdog Hawks upset Minnesota in Minneapolis and brought the bronze porker back to Iowa for the first time in five years. It was also the first time Iowa had won a road game in sixteen tries, going back to early in the 1965 season.

1976: Iowa 20, Minnesota 12

The Gophers went into the game heavily favored at home, sporting a 5–1 record, including 3–0 in the conference. But Iowa rallied from a 12–0 deficit in the second half, with Bill Schultz hauling in 2 touchdown passes, one for 70 yards from Butch Caldwell and the other a 28-yarder from Tom McLaughlin.

1986: Iowa 30, Minnesota 27

Who can forget the circumstances that decided this wild one? It was played before a Metrodome record crowd of 65,018, including some 15,000 Iowans, and appeared to end in a 27–27 tie when Iowa's Rob Houghtlin barely missed a last-second 51-yard field goal. But a penalty was called on Minnesota for having twelve players on the field, giving Iowa one more play and putting Houghtlin 15 yards closer to the uprights. He calmly booted that one straight down the middle for the winning points.

1997: Iowa 31, Minnesota 0

This was Tim Dwight's swan song in Kinnick Stadium, and he went out in a blaze of glory with 2 touchdowns, the first on a pass and the other on one of his typical electrifying punt returns. Dwight, a sprinter on the track team, set two Big Ten career records for punt returns: touchdowns (5) and total yards (1,086).

The Songs and the Bands

You had to live in Iowa midway through the last century to fully appreciate how much the natives developed a distaste for "The Iowa Corn Song." The tune itself wasn't so much the problem because it was lively and spirited, but the words that went along with it did not stand the test of time. They were, in a word, corny.

Although Iowans farm some of the richest land in the world and are happy to be from a state known as the nation's breadbasket, they don't take kindly to anything appearing to cast them in the image of hayseeds. They would much prefer to leave that to Hoosiers, as in Indiana. The first line in "The Iowa Corn Song" goes like this: "Let's sing of Grand old I-O-Way, I-O-Way," and that's a turnoff right there. As all good Iowans know, they live in I-O-W*ah*, not I-O-W*ay*.

The chorus, which is by far the most well-known part of the song, goes this way:

> *We're from I-O-Way, I-O-Way, State of all the land*
> *Joy on ev-ry hand. We're from I-O-Way, I-O-Way,*
> *That's where the tall corn grows.*

The words, put to the music of an old 1800s song called "Traveling," were written in 1912 by George Hamilton, who at the time was secretary of the Des Moines Chamber of Commerce and prominent in the Masonic Lodge, particularly among Shriners. It was while attending a national convention in Los Angeles that he decided Iowa's Shriners needed a rousing song that would also advertise the main product of their home state: corn.

Little did Hamilton realize how those lyrics would catch on and thrive over the years. Many verses were written and rewritten, but the chorus stayed intact and was played over and over at state and national events, ad nauseam some would say. If it wasn't the official state song, it certainly was the best known, and for a long time it became attached to the University of Iowa's athletic teams.

In about 1950, university officials felt they'd had enough and made written requests for bands in the conference (then the Big

A Band of Travelers

Join the Iowa band and see the country. Or another slogan might be: As the football team goes, so goes the band—sometimes from coast to coast. In 1987 the Hawkeyes opened their season playing in the Kickoff Classic at the Meadowlands in East Rutherford, New Jersey. They closed it at the Holiday Bowl in San Diego. The band went along on both trips.

If you were fortunate enough to be one of Iowa's musicians in 1991, you played twice in California that year. The 1990 season closed with a trip to the Rose Bowl, so the band marched in the parade and performed at the game on New Year's Day, 1991. The following December the team and band wound up the 1991 season back at the Holiday Bowl.

Before long it was off to the East Coast again. The 1992 season opened with another game in New Jersey's Kickoff Classic. All that is in addition to the band making one out-of-town trip every year during the regular season.

Nine) not to play "The Corn Song" as being representative of the Hawkeyes. But the trouble was, there wasn't a suitable alternative. The school's official march, "On Iowa," didn't have the same recognition and the words were not what you would call a fight song.

For a *Cedar Rapids Gazette* newspaper writer named Len Zacheis, the last straw came in October 1950 when he received a Percy Faith album of college songs in the mail. There it was again, making his skin crawl. In his record review column, Zacheis wrote, "Putting it bluntly, the University of Iowa and its athletic teams deserve a better rouser than the rickey-tickey tune that fate wished upon them. The 'Corn Song' may have been hot

The Iowa band pays tribute to coach Hayden Fry.

stuff in the days of the silver cornet band, but it's strictly from hunger today. Maybe if Meredith Willson keeps hammering away, he'll turn out a spirited, swingy state song fit for a university some day."

Willson, an Iowa native from Mason City, was a noted songwriter and bandleader who had written the highly successful Broadway musical *The Music Man.* Zacheis sent his column and an accompanying note to Willson, who took the plea to heart. A month later Willson wrote Zacheis that he had completed a new Iowa song, saying, "I hope the boys will like it, but if not, I'll try again."

The song aired for the first time on nationwide radio the following December 31, New Year's Eve, on NBC's *The Big Show*. Tallulah Bankhead, the mistress of ceremonies, said Willson and his band would play his new Iowa song as a salute to the Big Ten and the next day's Rose Bowl game.

These are the words to the catchy tune that all good Hawkeye fans have come to know:

The word is "Fight! Fight! Fight! for IOWA,"
Let every loyal Iowan sing.
The word is "Fight! Fight! Fight! for IOWA,"
Until the walls and rafters ring.

RAH! RAH!

Come on and cheer, cheer, cheer for IOWA,
Come on and cheer until you hear the final gun.
The word is "Fight! Fight! Fight! for IOWA,"
Until the game . . . is . . . won.

Meredith Willson attended Iowa's Rose Bowl game in 1982 and, just shy of his eightieth birthday, he directed the Hawkeye marching band in playing his song, doing it with joy and great verve before a crowd of 105,000.

The song was introduced to an Iowa audience February 12, 1951, at halftime of an Iowa-Indiana basketball game and was an instant success. It brought Iowa up to speed with the rest of the Big Ten schools, giving the Hawks a fight song all their own.

Some of the most inspirational and memorable college songs date from the early days of college football, such as Michigan's "Hail to the Victors," the "Notre Dame Victory March," "On Wisconsin," the "Minnesota Rouser," "Fight on for USC," and a

First Mascot Was a Bear

It's a little known fact that Iowa's first football mascot was a six-month-old bear cub who was found in the hills of Idaho in 1908 and brought to Iowa City, where he was housed in a cage under the bleachers at old Iowa Field. The players named him "Burch," and according to newspaper stories of that era, they referred to him as "one of the boys."

Burch was on the sidelines at all the home games in 1908 and 1909. He had a short life, however. He drowned in the adjacent Iowa River in the spring of 1910.

number of others. Iowa's "On Iowa" was an original tune with lyrics composed in 1917 by W. Robert Law, a University of Iowa law school graduate, class of 1904. He entered it in a contest in 1917 but it didn't win. There is no record of what happened to the winner, but two years later Law's "On Iowa" was adopted as the university's official song. The band still plays this in parades and football games about as often as it plays Willson's "Iowa Fight Song." These are the words:

> On, Iowa, proudly at the fore,
> On, Iowa, on forever more,
> Ev'ry loyal son will give a rousing toast to you,
> Ev'ry loyal daughter loves you true.
> On, Iowa, with your wealth untold,
> A heritage to us you did unfold,
> Love of family, love of friend,
> Love of country, too, makes us

Proud for what you stand,
Our dear Old Gold.

One other song demands to be mentioned, although it has no official status with Iowa, and for a while some university administrators sought to have the band stop playing it because the words promote beer drinking. That song is an old polka titled, "In Heaven There Is No Beer." There are literally dozens of verses to this snappy tune. Nobody is quite sure when the Iowa band started playing it, some time around 1970, but the song caught on and is now used to celebrate a Hawkeye football or basketball victory.

Over the years Iowa has had relatively few band directors, starting in 1911 with O. E. Van Doren, a dentist whose first love was music. He held the director's post for twenty-six years until being succeeded by C. B. Righter, who carried the baton for seventeen years.

In 1954, just as Forest Evashevski's Hawkeyes were starting to make their mark on the national level, Fred Ebbs came in to add a new direction and energetic leadership to the marching band. The musical beat became lively and up-tempo under Ebbs, more in keeping with the times, and when Iowa went to the Rose Bowl in 1957, the band put on an impressive performance in the New Year's Day parade and later at the game, when the football team whipped Oregon State.

Two years later the Hawks were back in the Rose Bowl again, this time routing California, and the *Pasadena Independent* offered these words of praise: "The Iowa band had the California blowers licked before they stepped on the field. Cal's band was good, too, but the Hawkeye tooters were better. The way they

Herky the Hawk

It wasn't until after World War II that Iowa came up with a symbol for its athletic teams. Richard Spencer III, a journalism instructor, spent some time studying hawks in the university's museum and then drew a cartoon character in 1948 that is now known as Herky the Hawk.

The Hawk was only a logo for several years until the athletic department held a statewide contest to give the impish bird a name. John Franklin, an alumnus from Belle Plaine, came up with the winning entry. Now the mascot is so popular that eight to ten students are needed at different times to play the role of Herky at athletic contests and numerous other events.

Herky fires up the crowd.

went about outclassing the opposition was as businesslike as that turned in by coach Evashevski's gridmen."

Ebbs left for another job in 1967 and was replaced by Tom Davis, not to be confused with the former Iowa basketball coach of the same name. Davis had a brief six-year term before leaving as band director to devote more time to his duties as head of the percussion department. Before departing in 1973, however, he made one important addition to the band—women.

Younger readers may find this surprising, but women were not allowed to become members of the marching band until 1972, except when they were needed to fill the ranks in the World War II years. Women who were in the band when the war ended were allowed to continue until they graduated, but after that it returned to an all-male club.

Morgan Jones, a former band member, took over as director in 1973 and an explosive growth pattern followed. In the next few years, the band doubled in size and now it numbers between 240 and 250 members. Also during Jones's time, an alumni band was formed and that's continued to grow, too. The old grads are one of the featured attractions each year at homecoming.

Myron Welch has been Iowa's director of bands for the last quarter century. Kevin Kostens is director of the marching band, and since this has been a period of great success for the football teams, nobody follows all the bowl talk with greater anticipation every year than do his musicians. They get to go, too. In addition to traveling to one Big Ten road game each season, the band has made eighteen bowl trips in the last twenty-four years.

Iowa had another musical group, the Scottish Highlanders, that long ago faded from the scene. It started as an all-male band of bagpipers and drummers in the 1930s, marching in parades and at football games, but switched to women during and after World War II. The Highlanders were popular for a number of years, even making several trips to Scotland, but when finances became a problem and interest waned, they were disbanded in 1980.

The Iowa State Rivalry

When a young football fan glances through scores of past Iowa–Iowa State games, it might be hard for him or her to understand why the two schools had such a long break in the series, a period lasting forty-three years from 1934 until the renewal began in 1977. Didn't they realize the revenue they were passing up? The game is almost always sold out. It's such a hot ticket that both universities charge more for the intrastate game than they do for others on their schedules.

Couldn't they see that the rivalry was something just about everyone in the state really cared about? It builds interest for both programs, leads to endless hours of coffee-time talk, friendly wagers, fierce competition on the field, bragging rights to the winner, and a year of anticipation for the next game to arrive.

The biggest problem is keeping a lid on the emotions, which has been done admirably in recent times but not so well in the early years. In fact, that's a good place to begin in understanding why the schools decided not to play each other for such a long time—in all sports, not just football—and why it finally took enormous pressure from the state legislature on the two university presidents before athletic relations were resumed in the 1970s.

Hard feelings developed in the early era of football, and so there were several breaks in the series. The first serious controversy happened in the 1897 game at Iowa City, when Iowa State's Foster Parker ran 40 yards for a touchdown in the last quarter, giving the Cyclones a 12–10 lead.

Iowa's players and coaches claimed one of their players had been fouled on the play, and when there was no penalty to nullify the score, they walked off the field and gave Iowa State a 6–0 forfeit decision. An Iowa City sportswriter got a bit carried away in describing what he thought of the officiating: "The umpire, whose sole duty it is to observe such things, says he failed to see the play," he wrote. "Why? Either because he did not want to see it, or because he was grossly, not to say criminally, negligent. We believe the latter to be the true explanation. That he is endowed with at least normal vision, and could see when he made an effort to do so, is attested to in his other numerous decisions, every one of which went against Iowa."

Iowa-Iowa State Series

Year	Winner	Score	Year	Winner	Score
1894	Iowa State	16-8	1979	Iowa	30-14
1895	Iowa State	24-0	1980	Iowa State	10-7
1897	Iowa State	6-0	1981	Iowa State	23-12
1899	Iowa	5-0	1982	Iowa State	19-7
1901	Iowa	12-0	1983	Iowa	51-10
1902	Iowa	12-6	1984	Iowa	59-21
1904	Iowa	10-6	1985	Iowa	57-3
1905	Iowa	8-0	1986	Iowa	43-7
1906	Iowa State	2-0	1987	Iowa	48-9
1907	Iowa State	20-14	1988	Iowa	10-3
1909	Iowa	16-0	1989	Iowa	31-21
1910	Iowa	2-0	1990	Iowa	45-35
1911	Iowa State	9-0	1991	Iowa	29-10
1912	Iowa	20-7	1992	Iowa	21-7
1913	Iowa	45-7	1993	Iowa	31-28
1914	Iowa	26-6	1994	Iowa	37-9
1915	Iowa State	16-0	1995	Iowa	27-10
1916	Iowa	19-16	1996	Iowa	38-13
1917	Iowa	6-3	1997	Iowa	63-20
1918	Iowa	21-10	1998	Iowa State	27-9
1919	Iowa	10-0	1999	Iowa State	17-10
1920	Iowa	14-10	2000	Iowa State	24-14
1933	Iowa	27-7	2001	Iowa State	17-14
1934	Iowa State	31-6	2002	Iowa State	36-31
1977	Iowa	12-10	2003	Iowa	40-21
1978	Iowa State	31-0	2004	Iowa	17-10

A cooling-off period seemed to be in order, and Iowa State did not appear on Iowa's schedule in 1898. There was a similar one-year interruption in 1908, after Iowa State admitted it had used an ineligible player while winning the 1907 game: one Thomas K. Willett, who had played two years at Grinnell, 1902–3, and then four more seasons for the Cyclones, 1904–7. Iowa State made a formal apology and the two schools were back at it in 1909. Iowa extracted a measure of revenge with a 16–0 victory, and the crowd of 5,500 was called the largest to see a game in Iowa City up to that time.

In 1916 the United States commissioner of higher education, P. P. Claxton, issued a report titled, *State of Higher Education Institutions of Iowa*, discussing general antagonisms between the two universities and urging an end to their football games. Thus, between 1920 and 1977 there would be only two meetings: Iowa's 27–7 triumph at home in 1933, and a huge upset by Iowa State in Ames the following year, 31–6. The schools reportedly could not agree on a date in 1935, and their presidents decided to discontinue the series indefinitely.

Over the years there would be occasional talk of a renewal, and even informal negotiations that proved fruitless in 1949, and it became mostly a one-way street: Iowa State seeking a resumption and Iowa deciding it had nothing to gain by playing the Cyclones (money and lots of it still wasn't in the picture). Iowa was the big kid on the block, with a stadium seating 53,000 compared to only 20,000 for Clyde Williams Field in Ames.

The state legislature attempted to intervene several times but with no success, although a resolution by Bill Reichardt of Des Moines, the former Hawkeye star, seemed to make some headway in 1965. It directed the Iowa and Iowa State presidents "to investigate the feasibility of arranging their football schedules to allow games to be played between the two schools as often and as soon as possible."

After a flurry of letters between the presidents and Reichardt, and between faculty representatives and athletic directors, it all came to naught with the release of an Iowa statement in September of 1965 that sang the same old tune: "The Board in Control of Athletics wishes to state again its belief that any activity, athletic or otherwise, which places the universities, their students, alumni, faculties, or their friends in opposition to one another should be discouraged as not in the best academic interests of the institutions of the State of Iowa."

Reichardt and others continued to apply the needle, however, and a major breakthrough came in 1968, when Iowa's athletic board authorized athletic director Forest Evashevski to begin talks with his counterpart at Iowa State, Clay Stapleton, about resuming the football series at some future date. Evy had come to the conclusion that he couldn't in good faith schedule games with other teams in Iowa State's conference—Nebraska, for example—without playing the Cyclones once in a while.

So that's how the first two games were agreed upon, in the 1977 and 1978 seasons, and officially announced in the fall of 1968. It was a banner-headline story, of course, and one year later four more games were added for 1979 through 1982; all six games were scheduled in Iowa City because of the larger stadium.

It sounds so simple, but all was not clear sailing from there. At the time those games were being negotiated, Evashevski was embroiled in a bitter dispute with his football coach, Ray Nagel. It became so heated that the athletic board relieved both men of

One for the Books

Iowa and Iowa State played a game at Ames in 1906 that wasn't much to watch, unless you liked defense and lots of kicking. The teams totaled just 3 first downs. There were 45 punts, 23 by Iowa's Maury Kent, who later was a longtime member of the Hawkeye athletic staff. The only score came when Iowa State blocked a punt that resulted in a safety and a 2–0 victory.

their duties in May 1970, allowing Evy to resign and firing Nagel, although he was later reinstated.

Bump Elliott, then an assistant athletic director at Michigan, was named to replace Evashevski, reporting to work on July 1, 1970. Then came another surprise. Iowa announced that it would play only the first two games against Iowa State and not the other four, claiming Evy had acted beyond his authority in scheduling them. The fact that the news media had long since announced the four-game addition was disregarded.

Iowa State cried foul, taking the matter to the board of regents. Well, the regents wanted no part of this hot potato. It hired an outside arbitrator to rule on the matter, and he determined that based on the correspondence between the schools and the announcements made in the newspapers, Iowa was morally obligated to play all six games, not just two.

A rider was placed in the second contract that should Iowa State build a stadium with a seating capacity in the 50,000 range, Iowa would consider moving one of the final two games to Ames. With the completion of Cyclone Stadium in 1975, now Jack

Trice Stadium, the 1981 game was switched to Ames, and since then the series has been played on a home-and-home basis.

There were a few more disputes to be resolved, such as the number of tickets that would be allotted to Iowa State as the visiting team in the early years. At first Iowa offered 1,500 as part of its standard contract ("You're joking!" screamed Iowa State officials), raised it to 5,000 ("Still not enough," they said), and then settled on 10,000. Once they'd reached an agreement on that, kickoff time finally arrived in Kinnick Stadium on September 17, 1977.

Finally! Some Iowans thought they'd never live to see the day. The advance buildup was probably unmatched in the state's history for any athletic event, and a sellout crowd of 57,725 turned out on a bright and sunny afternoon to sit in on the festivities. It was a tough ticket, too. The face value might have been $8.00—cheap in retrospect—but scalpers were getting $50.00 and up.

Iowa State was on the upswing under coach Earle Bruce in the mid-1970s, finishing with an 8–3 record in 1976, and was a slight favorite, ranking second nationally in total offense. Iowa had not had a winning season in sixteen years, but as always, hopes were high for improvement.

Following pregame warm-ups, Bruce took his squad to the visitors dressing room and handed each player a surprise gift, jerseys that were emblazoned with "Beat Iowa" across the front above the numbers. The Cyclones quickly changed jerseys and raced back onto the field for the opening kickoff. "That was one of the biggest mistakes I ever made in coaching," Bruce said years later. "It really backfired. There had already been plenty of hype and emotion about the game, and when the Iowa players saw those jerseys they got charged up all the more."

A 61-Point Turnaround

There have been some shocking results in the intrastate
series, but none more so than the game at Iowa City in 1998,
when the Cyclones ignored the odds-makers (they were 4-
touchdown underdogs) and posted a convincing 27-9 victory.
That's a 61-point turnabout from the year before. Iowa won the
1997 game in Ames, 63-20, to set a series scoring record.

Two freshmen did most of the quarterbacking: Bob
Commings Jr., son of Iowa's head coach, for the Hawks; and John
Quinn for Iowa State. As might be expected, with so much excite-
ment plus the rookie leadership on both sides, the game was far
from a classic. An impartial observer doubtless wondered what all
the fuss was about.

Iowa managed only 6 first downs and Iowa State 8. All the
scoring was crammed into about seven minutes midway through
the first half, with Iowa pulling off an upset, 12–10, on Dennis
Mosley's 77-yard touchdown run and Jon Lazar's short return of
a fumble recovery. The Cyclones scored on a 63-yard punt return
by Tom Buck and a field goal by Scott Kollman.

Iowa State got its revenge the following season by rolling to a
31–0 victory behind the quarterbacking of a junior-college
transfer, Walter Grant. He threw for 3 touchdowns to give the
Cyclones their widest winning margin in the ancient series.

Coach Hayden Fry used to get particularly fired up for games against Iowa State.

After the first two games had generated so much enthusiasm, Iowa's administrators realized what they'd been missing out on all those years. Before the third game of the renewal, the two athletic directors, Elliott and Iowa State's Lou McCullough, met in the office of Iowa governor Robert Ray and signed a contract to extend the series through 1987. That was tantamount to saying the series was a permanent fixture.

New coaches were at the helm in 1979, Hayden Fry replacing Commings and Donnie Duncan taking over at Iowa State after Bruce left for Ohio State. Fry's team lost its first three games that season before he notched his first Hawkeye victory by beating the Cyclones, 30–14, with Mosley lugging the ball 39 times for 229 yards and 3 touchdowns.

Then the Alex Giffords Era began at Iowa State. Giffords was a talented placekicker who totaled 8 field goals in his career against Iowa, including 4 in one game, and his kicks furnished the winning margin three years in a row. After that, however, it would be many long years before Cyclone fans had much to cheer about.

Iowa, however, was entering one of the most successful periods in school history and thoroughly dominated the intrastate series by winning fifteen straight games from 1983 to 1997, many by lopsided scores. The stars of the show in those years were quarterback Chuck Long, who passed for 684 yards and 8 touchdowns while leading the Hawks to victories in 1983, 1984, and 1985; and a pair of speed merchants in the 1990s, running back Tavian Banks and wide receiver Tim Dwight.

Banks scored 9 touchdowns against the Cyclones in his four-year career at Iowa from 1994 through 1997. Dwight always seemed to be doing something spectacular, whether it was turning a short pass into a long gain or sprinting to the end zone on a punt return. In the 1997 Iowa State game, when Iowa won by a record 63–20 score, Dwight caught 8 passes for 187 yards and 3 touchdowns.

"I never coached a player I enjoyed more than Tim Dwight," said Fry. "He was so full of energy and inspiration that he made everyone around him better and made the game a lot more fun."

Thanks to Fry's record, sixteen victories in twenty meetings, Iowa has built a substantial lead in the series. After the 2004 season, the Hawks owned a 19–9 advantage since the start of the renewal and an overall lead of 35–17 going back to when the schools first met in 1894.

Two of Fry's former assistants have taken charge of the rival programs in recent years, Dan McCarney directing Iowa State to five straight victories in the series from 1998 to 2002, and Kirk Ferentz winning the 2003 and 2004 games for Iowa. Ferentz's streak has to end sometime, but going into the 2005 season, his Hawkeyes had won eighteen consecutive home games since a 36–31 loss to Iowa State in 2002.

Rose Bowl Memories

Randy Duncan became a celebrity at Iowa as an All-America quarterback in 1958 and pro football's number one draft choice by the Green Bay Packers, but to his teammates he will never be forgotten for something else: his legendary kisses with two movie stars in Hollywood. First it was a blonde bombshell, Jayne Mansfield. Then it was a ravishing redhead, Rhonda Fleming. A young guy can't do much better than that.

For many years comedian Bob Hope put together a variety show to entertain Big Ten teams at a Dinner for Champions two nights before the Rose Bowl game. The Big Ten Club of Southern California sponsored the banquet, and part of Hope's pay would be several hundred tickets to the game that he could pass out to friends. "Before we left for Pasadena in 1956," recalled Duncan, who was a sophomore quarterback at the time, "we were asked to fill out a questionnaire about what we wanted to do in California. Most of the guys put down stuff like, 'I want a victory over Oregon State,' but I put down, 'I want a date with Jayne Mansfield.' I didn't think any more about it, but at the Big Ten dinner with Bob Hope, Jayne Mansfield actually showed up. And they called me up on the stage to meet her."

A Rare Rose Bowl Double

Iowa's football-playing Happels, father and son, claim an unusual distinction in the history of bowl games. It hasn't been done often, if at all. Each scored a touchdown in the Rose Bowl twenty-nine years apart.

Papa Bill had a 5-yard scoring run when the Hawks beat Oregon State in 1957. Son Bill matched that by catching an 11-yard touchdown pass from Chuck Long in the 1986 game, which the Hawkeyes lost to UCLA.

"That really tickled me when he got his," said the elder Happel, an Iowa City businessman who was a spectator at the game. "Billy outdid just about everything I ever accomplished, except we won our game. That's the only thing I have over him."

Duncan did not waste the opportunity to do more than say hello. He took the blonde beauty in his arms and gave her a long smooch, with a roar of approval from his Hawkeye teammates. "I was the envy of all the guys on the team," he said.

Iowa beat Oregon State, 35–19, with Duncan playing the second quarter after the starting quarterback, Kenny Ploen, was sidelined with an injured knee. Ploen, who had run 49 yards for an early touchdown, wasn't seriously hurt. He returned in the second half and played so well he was voted the game's most valuable player.

Two years later Duncan led a high-powered offense that shattered a number of Rose Bowl records while routing California, 38–12. The Hawks piled up 516 yards in total offense, including 429 rushing with Bob Jeter accounting for 194 on just 9 carries. Jeter set one of the records with an 81-yard scoring run, and his spectacular sophomore running mate, Willie Fleming, had 2 touchdowns—the fifth consecutive game in which he'd done that. Fleming's career was a short one, however, because he flunked out of school the next semester.

Duncan vividly recalls two parties that are at the top of his Pasadena memory list, one before and one after that game. The first was the Big Ten dinner again, where Rhonda Fleming made an appearance and said she'd heard there was a budding screen lover in the crowd. She called Duncan up on the stage, and, sure enough, he didn't disappoint his whistling teammates.

The other party was in Duncan's room back at the hotel after the game, where many of the players congregated to celebrate the victory. They ordered room service well into the night. As each supply of food and beverages arrived, the players toasted assistant coach Bob Flora. It was Flora's room number that they kept signing to the tab. "The bill was huge," said Duncan. "Flora wasn't too happy with us."

Duncan spurned the NFL, incidentally, something that just wouldn't happen today with number one draft choices and their instant millions of dollars. Instead, he played several years for Vancouver of the Canadian Football League while going to law school, then returned to Des Moines and entered private practice.

Ploen had preceded Duncan into the Canadian league, enjoying a great career by leading the Winnipeg Blue Bombers to three Grey Cup titles. He's been inducted into the CFL Hall of Fame, the Manitoba Hall of Fame, and won many big games and other awards, but ask him what his career highlight was and he'll quickly say the Rose Bowl. "There's no question, it was the all-time high as far as I was concerned," he said. "It's something one dreams about, growing up in Iowa, and when it comes to be, it's a pretty big deal. The trip brings back nothing but good memories. Evy took us out early—well before Christmas—and gave us plenty of time to see all the sights."

Like so many others, he fondly remembers the Big Ten dinner and Bob Hope's humor. Hope would always huddle with his writers beforehand to put together a few topical jokes about whatever team he was going to entertain. At the 1956 dinner he wowed the Hawks with this line: "The first time I heard the name Forest Evashevski, I thought it was a national park in Russia."

At the same gathering before the 1959 game, Hope told the audience, "You know, California is already protesting this game. That's right, they've lodged a protest because Iowa has Mac Lewis listed as one player." Lewis, a 6'6", 305-pound tackle, might not be unusual now, but he was gigantic for players of that era.

Iowa's Bowl Games

1957	Rose Bowl:	Iowa 35, Oregon State 19
1959	Rose Bowl:	Iowa 38, California 12
1982	Rose Bowl:	Washington 28, Iowa 0
1982	Peach Bowl:	Iowa 28, Tennessee 22
1983	Gator Bowl:	Florida 14, Iowa 6
1984	Freedom Bowl:	Iowa 55, Texas 17
1986	Rose Bowl:	UCLA 45, Iowa 28
1986	Holiday Bowl:	Iowa 39, San Diego State 38
1987	Holiday Bowl:	Iowa 20, Wyoming 19
1988	Peach Bowl:	North Carolina State 28, Iowa 23
1991	Rose Bowl:	Washington 46, Iowa 34
1991	Holiday Bowl:	Iowa 13, Brigham Young 13
1993	Alamo Bowl:	California 37, Iowa 3
1995	Sun Bowl:	Iowa 38, Washington 18
1996	Alamo Bowl:	Iowa 27, Texas Tech 0
1997	Sun Bowl:	Arizona State 17, Iowa 7
2001	Alamo Bowl:	Iowa 19, Texas Tech 16
2003	Orange Bowl:	Southern California 38, Iowa 17
2004	Outback Bowl:	Iowa 37, Florida 17
2005	Capital One Bowl:	Iowa 30, Louisiana State 25

Hope's popularity with Big Ten teams spanned the generations, too, much like his foreign tours to entertain U.S. armed forces over the decades. Although it was more than twenty years before Iowa returned to the Rose Bowl for a third time, the players on Hayden Fry's 1981 squad raved about the Big Ten dinner, thanks in large part to Hope's comedy. "That's something I'll never forget," said Bob Stoops, an All–Big Ten defensive back for the Hawks and now Oklahoma's head coach. "It was such a classy production, and then to have somebody of Bob Hope's stature entertaining you—that was really great. After it was over, he hung around our bus and visited with all the players. What a class person he was, and what a great event that is."

Stoops said he had a special feeling of accomplishment making it to Pasadena in Hayden Fry's third season at Iowa because the conference co-championship was so unexpected. But then came the game, a 28–0 loss to Washington, which got a career performance from freshman running back Jacque Robinson: 142 yards rushing and 2 touchdowns. The Hawks also contributed to their downfall with 5 turnovers. "I don't think any of us realized what a disappointment it would be to lose it," says Stoops. "Everyone thought getting there was great and whatever happens now would be icing on the cake. But it took an awful lot away losing it."

That goes in spades for Iowa's 45–28 loss to UCLA in the 1986 Rose Bowl. The Hawks had one of their greatest teams ever in 1985, ranked number one nationally five weeks in a row, and they were favored to win, but what happened to them was not unlike what befell the 1981 team. Once again, they turned the ball over 5 times, and once again they could not stop an unheralded freshman running back, Eric Ball. He scored 4 touchdowns while running for 227 yards in 22 carries.

One of the mysteries of that game was how Iowa's usually sure-handed running back, Ronnie Harmon, could fumble the ball away 4 times—all in the first half. He'd never done anything like that before, fumbling only once all season. He personally tied a Rose Bowl record, since no team had lost more than 4 fumbles before, but he also matched another mark with 11 pass catches, something that got lost in the shuffle because of all the

Iowa's marching band performs at the 1986 Rose Bowl game in Pasadena.

miscues. "It's just one of those things," a dejected Harmon said afterwards. "I didn't plan to fumble. You know, I think you have to give UCLA some credit for causing the fumbles. They kept stripping me of the ball. They must try to do that all the time, and they sure do a good job of it."

Cynics immediately wondered if the game had been fixed by the gamblers, but there was never any evidence of that, and Harmon's teammates think any such talk is implausible. "Sure, the turnovers killed us," says Jay Norvell, a defensive back on that team and now an assistant coach at Nebraska. "But that's not the way I remember Ronnie Harmon. To me, Ronnie Harmon is pretty close to being the best football player I've ever seen. He did things that I didn't think anybody could do on a football field. I would go to war with Ronnie Harmon any day. He just had one of those days. It's too bad it had to happen in such a big game."

One player who could immediately sympathize with Harmon's plight was the team's brilliant quarterback, Chuck Long, whose 4 pass interceptions at Ohio State proved costly in Iowa's only loss of the regular season. "I really feel sorry for him," Long said a day after the game. "I've been in the same position, so I know how he feels. I felt terrible after turning the ball over 4 times at Ohio State, but at least I had a couple more weeks to redeem myself. He doesn't have that opportunity."

When Hayden Fry wrote an autobiography wrapping up his long coaching career, titled *Hayden Fry, a High Porch Picnic*, he said Harmon had never been a fumbler and that's why his play that day was so uncharacteristic. Like Harmon, Fry felt UCLA had a lot to do with the butterfingers. "The game film reveals that every fumble he lost was caused by a UCLA defender making a hard hit," the coach said. "They just knocked the ball loose. They did a great job of tackling. UCLA made bad things happen to Iowa; Iowa didn't self-destruct. Ronnie Harmon had a tremendous football career with the Hawkeyes, and I hated to see it end that way."

Something else occurred in the 1986 game that was overshadowed by all the mistakes, yet it had long-lasting effects for one of Iowa's all-time great defensive players, linebacker Larry Station. He suffered a back injury in the first half and it turned out to be a herniated disc, which required surgery the following spring. Station was drafted by the Pittsburgh Steelers, but the bad back dashed his dreams of a career in pro football.

Iowa fielded another star-studded lineup in 1990 with seven All–Big Ten players, led by the conference's most valuable

Hayden Fry brought Iowa to national prominence and to a string of bowl appearances.

player, powerful running back Nick Bell, and standout quarterback Matt Rodgers. The Hawks did the unthinkable that season in sharing the Big Ten title with Michigan State, Michigan, and Illinois. Iowa and those three teams finished with 6–2 conference records—the only four-way championship tie in Big Ten history—but the Hawks got the Rose Bowl nod because they'd beaten the other three teams—all on the road—in a period of just five weeks.

The 12–7 victory at Michigan State was only a mild upset, with linebacker Melvin Foster recording 20 tackles, but the other two were against teams ranked in the Top Ten. Iowa rallied in the last quarter to edge number eight Michigan in Ann Arbor, 24–23, and two weeks later destroyed number five Illinois in Champaign, 56–24, in a stunning form reversal. The Illini boasted the nation's third-ranked defense at the time, but you would never know it by what happened that day. Iowa jumped out to a 28–0 lead in the first quarter and cruised to victory, with Bell and teammate Tony Stewart each rushing for more than 100 yards.

So it was back to the Rose Bowl to face Washington's Pac-10 champions; unfortunately, it was the same song, third verse, for Fry and his troops. Iowa turned the ball over 5 times—why does that have a familiar ring?—and Washington blitzed the Hawks,

He Wore Many Hats

When former Iowa athletic director Bump Elliott was named to the Rose Bowl Hall of Fame, he owned a unique distinction. He went to the Rose Bowl in five different capacities: as an All–Big Ten halfback on the Michigan team that beat Southern California in 1948, as an Iowa assistant coach, as a Michigan head coach, as a Michigan assistant athletic director, and finally as Iowa's athletic director.

46–34, after building an overwhelming 33–7 lead at halftime.

There are no warm remembrances from that game, but Iowa did get a consolation prize of sorts: a listing in the Rose Bowl record book that is still there. Washington and Iowa combined for the most points in the history of the "Granddaddy of Them All."

One pleasant memory shared by all Hawkeye bowl participants is the support they've received from their loyal and vocal followers wherever they've gone. The fans are known far and wide as the "bumblebees" because of the way they proudly deck themselves out in the school colors, and they almost took over southern California when they swarmed into town in the days leading up to the Rose Bowl games. "Everywhere we went, whether it was Disneyland, Knotts Berry Farm, or Universal Studios, we'd see Hawkeye fans dressed in their black and gold," remembered Scott Helverson, a wide receiver who made both trips in the 1980s. "There were thousands upon thousands of them at the games. We couldn't have had better support in Kinnick Stadium. Even though we lost to Washington in 1982, I'll never forget how loudly the Hawk fans were cheering for us at the end of the game. I think they felt it was such an accomplishment for us just getting there, they wanted to make sure we knew how much they appreciated it."

The strong fan following is one reason why Iowa is so attractive to bowl scouts. The Hawkeyes "travel well," as they say, meaning they bring a lot of tourist dollars, and that support has grown steadily over the years, no matter where the bowl game is played. An estimated 10,000 Iowans attended the 1957 and 1959 Rose Bowl games, and up to 20,000 or so attended in the 1980s. That figure rose to 30,000 or more for their three straight trips to Florida early in the new century.

Kirk Ferentz— Making History

One of the first things Iowa athletic director Bob Bowlsby did when the regular season ended in 2004 was to tear up Kirk Ferentz's contract and give the forty-nine-year-old coach a new one, extending it through 2012 at a guaranteed annual package of $1.6 million.

The quick move was both a reward for what Ferentz had accomplished—being named the Big Ten Coach of the Year for the second time in three years—and also to head off the usual rumors about coaching vacancies and what it

Ferentz's Record at Iowa

	All Games		Conference	
	Wins	Losses	Wins	Losses
1999	1	10	0	8
2000	3	9	3	5
2001	7	5	4	4
2002	11	2	8	0
2003	10	3	5	3
2004	10	2	7	1

would take to lure the Hawkeye coach away. His most likely move figured to be as a head coach in the National Football League, where he'd been an assistant for a number of years.

Even Ferentz himself admitted after the 2003 season that he'd had serious discussions with the Jacksonville Jaguars about their coaching position. Pro teams can offer a jackpot that many colleges can't afford to match, although those deals come with risky job security. Ferentz's interest at that time was beyond Bowlsby's comfort level.

So, well before the 2004 season came to a close, Bowlsby huddled with his coach to work out a long-term contract extension. With bonuses and incentives the deal might soar into the $2 million range in some years. It was ready to be signed and sealed as soon as the season ended. "I couldn't be more pleased with it," said Bowlsby. "I think Kirk exemplifies everything that is good about college athletics. Our program is on a very solid base right

Kirk Ferentz coached Iowa to three successive January bowl games in 2003, 2004, and 2005.

Striking It Rich

Iowa coach Kirk Ferentz has various financial incentives built into his long-term contract. One of them encourages him to see that a good share of his players graduate. An annual graduation rate of 70 percent or higher will net him an extra $75,000.

There are numerous other possibilities for additional cash, including $175,000 for an outright Big Ten title or undefeated conference season; $100,000 for a shared title; $100,000 for a top twenty-five national finish, or $125,000 if it's the top twenty, and going up as high as $275,000 for the top five and $500,000 for the national championship; $175,000 for a Bowl Championship Series game; and $75,000 for playing in a bowl game with a $1 million payout or higher.

now. We obviously are paying a lot of money, but I feel it's a terrific bargain for our university."

That was a far cry from the way some fans felt when Ferentz (pronounced FAIR-intz) was hired in 1999 to replace his old mentor, Hayden Fry. They thought Bowlsby had bungled an opportunity to land Bob Stoops, a former Hawkeye star and another Fry alumnus, who had earned fame as an up-and-coming assistant coach at Kansas State and Florida. Whether he was spurned or not is a moot point now, but Stoops signed on as Oklahoma's head coach the night before Ferentz was interviewed at Iowa. In the eyes of many Iowa boosters, it appeared that the Hawkeyes had settled for the wrong man.

How do you think they felt when Ferentz's first team went 1–10 in 1999? Or in 2000, a modest improvement at 3–9, while

Stoops was winning the national championship at Oklahoma?

Bowlsby found himself inundated with angry e-mails and letters. It was not a happy situation for the athletic director or his coach. Even some of Ferentz's assistants came under fire with accusations that they were out of their league coaching in the Big Ten. The Hawkeye Internet chat rooms made for interesting reading, to say the least.

Then came a steady turnaround in 2001, featuring an early-season victory at Penn State and an overall 7–5 record, climaxed by a 19–16 upset of Texas Tech in the Alamo Bowl. From there the next three years were magical for Iowa fans: successive seasons of 11–2, 10–3, and 10–2; three straight number eight finishes in the national polls; and three January bowl games. The Hawkeyes had enjoyed only three ten-win seasons in the previous century.

The capper to this success story came on New Year's Day of 2005 when Iowa stunned Louisiana State University in the Capital One Bowl, 30–25, on an astounding touchdown pass as time expired. After LSU had seized the lead with only 46 seconds remaining, 25–24, Iowa quarterback Drew Tate lofted a high, arching pass that Warren Holloway ran under and hauled in for a scoring play covering 56 yards.

About half the sellout crowd of 70,229 erupted in joyous jubilation. Those were the estimated 30,000 delirious Iowa fans, who could scarcely believe what they had just witnessed. The other half could only sit there in quiet disbelief. Those were the LSU fans, whose celebration had been so rudely interrupted.

Holloway was an unlikely hero—a fifth-year senior from Homewood, Illinois, who had not caught a touchdown pass in his Hawkeye career. That Iowa even played in a New Year's Day bowl game was a testament to Ferentz's brilliant handiwork. He'd

Outland Trophy winner Robert Gallery waves an Iowa flag after the Hawkeyes' victory over Florida in the Outback Bowl.

been voted national Coach of the Year in 2002, guiding the underdog Hawkeyes into the Orange Bowl as part of the Bowl Championship Series, where they lost to the University of Southern California, 38–17. He proved that season was no fluke in 2003, with a rebuilt team that walloped Florida in the Outback Bowl, 37–17.

But what Ferentz accomplished in 2004 was the best of all, especially when you consider that his top four running backs went out with injuries almost before a Big Ten game had been played (three of them out for the season). A nonconference whipping at Arizona State, 44–7, made for a sorry outlook. The rushing attack was nonexistent—last among 117 Division I-A teams by the end of the season—but the Hawks still managed to tie for the conference championship.

They did it with the deadly passing of Tate, chosen for the all-conference team after a truly amazing sophomore year, and a solid defense that usually kept things close (despite what that Arizona State score indicates). Victories over Penn State, Purdue, and Minnesota were each by two points. Field goals by sophomore place-kicker Kyle Schlicher furnished the decisive points in all three: 2 in a crazy 6–4 win at Penn State, 3 to help beat Purdue 23–21, and a school-record 5 when the Hawks outscored Minnesota, 29–27.

End Matt Roth, tackle Jonathan Babineaux, and linebackers Chad Greenway and Abdul Hodge were the ringleaders of a defense that ranked in the top ten nationally. All four made the all-conference first team.

Iowa's four Hall of Fame coaches knew how to keep the old grads happy, by winning far more homecoming games than they

Goal Posts Come Down at Kinnick Stadium North

There is a reason why the Metrodome in Minneapolis has become known as Kinnick Stadium North when Iowa plays at Minnesota every other year. Hawkeye fans usually make up almost half the crowd. When Iowa completed its perfect Big Ten season at Minnesota in 2002, the Hawks had the support of some 25,000 to 30,000 fans. As soon as the game ended, with Iowa an easy 45–21 winner, many of them surged onto the field and ripped down the goal posts.

It was a crazy scene: opposing fans celebrating on a rival's field. One of the posts was torn apart and some revelers even carried a pole up an aisle of the indoor arena in an attempt to get away with a souvenir. Bad move. It led to a new Iowa-Minnesota joke: Only an Iowan would try to get a 20-foot pole out a revolving door. The Iowa athletic department sent the Gophers $5,000 to pay for the damage.

lost. Well, Ferentz had gone them one better. He just didn't lose at home, period. By the end of the 2004 season, his teams had won eighteen straight games in Kinnick Stadium. A string of thirteen consecutive home Big Ten victories starting in 2001 was the longest in school history.

Ferentz credits Iowa's noisy fans in the close confines of Kinnick Stadium as being instrumental to the team's success. All six home games were sold out in 2004 for an average crowd of 70,397—another school record. "Kinnick reminds me of a good, old-fashioned high school gym," said Ferentz. "You know, where the guy is standing taking the ball in bounds, and you have to say, 'Excuse me, can you move your legs, I have to take the ball in?' It's great."

But not for the visitors, of course. Kirk Herbstreit, a former Ohio State quarterback and now an ESPN analyst, knows all about that. "When Iowa is winning, this is the toughest place to play in the Big Ten," he said.

Ferentz recalled the time he spoke at a clinic in Las Vegas. "The guy picking me up at the airport had played for Minnesota. He was a punter. He got to talking about what a dreadful experience it was to be on Minnesota's bench for the course of a game. And I'm thinking, 'That's nice.'"

There is no better indication of Ferentz's coaching skill and his ability to adapt to his players than the fact that he took Iowa to four straight bowl games with different quarterbacks. First it was Kyle McCann in 2001, followed by Brad Banks, Nate Chandler, and now Tate.

The 6', 185-pound Tate was a prolific passer in high school at Baytown, Texas. After a year in which he played little as Chandler's backup, he hit the Big Ten by storm in 2004, ranking second in passing efficiency and third in total offense.

In addition to the accuracy of his right arm, Tate has a rare instinct for what is best described as "escapability," somehow eluding onrushing tacklers to avoid being sacked while giving him time to spot an open receiver. He threw for over 300 yards in four of the eight conference games.

Big Ten coaches are duly impressed, although they naturally don't like the prospect of facing him for two more years. "The thing I like about Drew Tate is that he's so tough and so compet-

Quarterback Drew Tate
had an outstanding
sophomore season in
2004.

itive," says Ohio State coach Jim Tressell. "I don't care what year you are, if you are those two things you succeed." Michigan coach Lloyd Carr also had high praise and said, "He's smart, he's an excellent thrower, and he creates plays. I think he's going to be one of the best quarterbacks in the country. He has a tremendous upside."

One man who deserves a lot of credit for building a potent attack around Tate—after the loss of all the running backs—is the team's offensive coordinator, Ken O'Keefe. The Hawkeye successes have to be a great source of satisfaction for O'Keefe, who was the object of many of the brickbats during the down years of 1999–2000. Some of his biggest fans now were among his harshest critics then.

By 2001 Iowa boasted the highest scoring offense in the Big Ten, even though the team barely scraped out a 6–5 record before winning in the Alamo Bowl, and it was obvious that O'Keefe must have been doing something right. He silenced the boobirds then and they haven't been heard from since.

Ferentz has made sure that O'Keefe, veteran defensive coordinator Norm Parker, and the rest of his Hawkeye staff will share

The Bowl Record

Iowa did not enjoy much good fortune in its last three Rose Bowl appearances, losing twice to Washington and once to UCLA, but the thrilling finish in the 2005 Capital One Bowl made up for some of that. The victory kept the Hawks well above .500 in bowl games, with an overall record of 11-8-1.

in the wealth. One stipulation in his new contract sets aside $175,000 to be distributed by Ferentz to nine assistants and two strength coaches. They also will receive an 8 percent pay boost after any season that Iowa goes to a bowl game and achieves a team graduation rate of 55 percent or higher in the most recent four-year period.

Although Ferentz is Iowa's top-paid state employee, he says his decision to stay put never was about the money but rather about enjoying the lifestyle of a college town like Iowa City and the relaxed atmosphere—as opposed to a more stressful situation in the pros. "This isn't a bad place," points out Ferentz, who was on Hayden Fry's staff for nine years in the 1980s. "I'm not the smartest guy in the world, but I figured that out a while ago. I can go elsewhere for more money, but it's not about that. My family and I have fifteen years invested here now. I can't imagine being in a better situation."

About the Author

Buck Turnbull, a graduate of the University of Iowa, covered Hawkeyes football for forty-one years as a sportswriter for the *Des Moines Register*. He was twice voted Iowa's Sportswriter of the Year. He also wrote the book *From the Press Box*.